Where the Ocean Sings

The World's Most Beautiful Beaches and Magical Bays

By
Alana Maren Bayside

Where the Ocean Sings

The World's Most Beautiful Beaches and Magical Bays

Table of Contents

Introduction

There's something about the call of the ocean that stirs a sense of wonder and adventure deep within us. The rhythmic lapping of waves against the shore and the whispering breeze that dances across the sand have long beckoned travelers to the world's coasts. A beach is more than just the meeting place of land and sea; it's a sanctuary, a canvas on which nature paints its most vivid canvases. This book is your invitation to explore the secluded paradises where the land caresses the sea's edge — a journey into coastal realms that promise serenity, inspiration, and awe.

Our planet is adorned with countless beaches, each with its own story and charm. Yet, not all beaches are created equal. Some are bustling with vibrant energy and the hustle of beachgoers, while others remain untouched sanctuaries, waiting to be discovered by those willing to venture off the beaten path. These hidden gems are the focus of our exploration, offering not only stunning natural beauty but also a chance to connect deeply with the pristine environment.

Adventure awaits those who dare to seek these clandestine corners of the earth. From the verdant cliffs of the Pacific Northwest to the tropical idylls of Polynesia, each destination holds a promise of discovery. Whether you're drawn to the vibrant undersea worlds populated by coral and vibrant marine life or captivated by the quiet elegance of a starlit sky reflected on tranquil waters, our journey will guide you through varied landscapes and experiences.

The allure of coastal escapes isn't merely in their physical beauty. It's the stories they whisper to those who listen — legends carried on the salt-sprayed breeze, myths echoed in the crash of distant waves. These narratives have traveled through time, shaping cultures and lives around them. With every grain of sand and every tide that rises, there's a story waiting to unfold, and you're invited to become part of it.

This book endeavors to go beyond the sandy shores. It's a celebration of the spirit of exploration and the transformative power of the sea. The ocean doesn't merely promise relaxation. It offers an opportunity to heal, to reflect, and to find clarity among nature's rhythms. We'll explore beaches that heal the mind, revealing the science behind why these gentle landscapes have such a profound impact on our well-being.

Inspiration flows from those who've walked these coasts before us. Travelers, poets, and artists have long found their muse here, where the sea meets the shore. Their tales will accompany us, providing not just insight but also a sense of shared journeying. Perhaps you'll discover your own creative spark sparked by a coastal sunrise or the tireless whispers of the ocean.

With each chapter, we'll steer through different regions of our world. From the mystical bays of Greece to the secluded strands of Australasia, each chapter explores unique facets of coastal beauty and the diverse cultures nurtured by the sea. Alongside these narratives will come practical guidance, offering tips for uncovering hidden spots and traveling responsibly to minimize your footprint on these delicate environments.

This introduction marks the first step in your exploration, an adventure that ventures beyond postcards and tourist maps into the soul of coastal paradises. As you turn these pages, you'll uncover the secrets of tide and time, experiencing the magic that these secluded shores have to offer. Welcome to a journey that promises both discovery and rediscovery — of captivating places and of oneself.

The coastlines of our planet invite us into a dialogue. It's a timeless conversation between humanity and the sea, a bond forged from ancient rhythms. As we embark on this odyssey, we embrace the wisdom offered by waves, winds, and sands. So join us, not just as a traveler, but as an explorer and a keeper of these stories, helping to protect and cherish the sacred spaces that inspire and enrich our lives.

Chapter 1:
The Allure of Coastal Escapes

There's a magnetism to the coastline, a romantic pull that stirs something deep within. Coastal escapes whisper promises of serene horizons, playful shores, and adventures into the unknown, evoking images of sun-drenched sands and the symphonic crashing of waves. It's an undeniable allure, a seductive charm, that calls travelers seeking both tranquility and thrill. Imagine standing at the edge of the world, where the ocean meets the sky, and feeling the salt-kissed breeze wrap around you like a gentle embrace. These paradises inspire wanderlust, bringing a sense of freedom that only the expanse of open water can impart. From quiet bays that capture your heart with their secluded beauty to vast stretches of beach that invite endless exploration, the world's coastal gems offer retreat and renewal, a place to discover both the world and oneself anew.

Beaches That Inspire Wanderlust

Imagine a place where the sand feels like powder under your feet, and the horizon stretches into infinity. Such beaches exist, quietly beckoning wanderers with their untouched beauty and promise of adventure. They are the shores that whisper stories of the world, calling travelers to experience their magic firsthand. Each beach has a soul, a rhythm that beats in time with the waves crashing onto the shore.

What is it about a beach that steals the breath away? It might be the way the colors change as daylight dances upon the water or the serenity found in the quiet corners of the coast. From the secluded coves to the sweeping expanses, every beach has its unique allure that entices explorers from around the globe. Some find solace in the silence of dawn walks along the shoreline, with only the rhythmic rush of the sea for company. Others seek the thrill of turquoise waves and the exhilaration of discovering an unspoiled paradise.

Let your mind wander to Anse Source d'Argent, one of the most photographed beaches in the world, located on La Digue Island in the Seychelles. This beach, with its pink-hued sands and striking granite boulders, is a masterpiece carved by nature. As you stand there, time seems to falter, entranced by the ethereal beauty that feels almost otherworldly. The waters are so clear that you feel as though you're hovering over an endless aquarium teeming with life.

Equally captivating is Navagio Beach in Greece, accessible only by boat and flanked by towering limestone cliffs that open up to reveal a hidden cove. Known as Shipwreck Beach due to the rusting remains of a freight ship nestled in its sands, this isolated paradise is surrounded by azure waters that seem to shimmer with secrets of the past.

In stark contrast, consider the windswept drama of Reynisfjara Beach in Iceland, where black sands meet the icy waters of the Atlantic. Towering basalt columns, known as Reynisdrangar, punctuate the seascape like mythical sentinels. It's a place where folklore thrives, and one can almost hear whispers of ancient sagas carried on the wind. The starkness of the landscape, with its moody skies and rugged beauty, captivates dreamers and daring adventurers alike, leaving an indelible mark on their souls.

The beaches of the Amalfi Coast in Italy offer a romantic contrast, inviting visitors to soak up the sun against a backdrop of colorful villages clinging to cliffs. Each beach in this region tells a story of history, of empires long past and the enduring magnetism of the Mediterranean. Wander along the shores of Positano, where the scent of lemon groves mingles with the ocean breeze, and feel life's chaos diminish in the mesmerizing rhythm of the waves.

For those in search of something more whimsical and adventurous, the beaches of Thailand provide a fascinating tapestry of life and nature. Railay Beach in Krabi, accessible only by boat due to the high limestone cliffs cutting off mainland access, offers an escape into an idyllic landscape where rock climbers tackle cliffs and snorkelers explore vibrant coral reefs beneath the wave's surface. The lush jungle that borders its white sands is home to curious monkeys and the occasional wanderer who's chosen to stay a bit longer than planned.

Something inexplicably transformative happens when visiting these shores that inspire wanderlust. It's not just the lure of picturesque scenery, but the reflection they invite, the stories they tell, and the moments of clarity they provide. Whether on a sprawling coast where the land meets the horizon or an intimate crescent of beach hidden from the world, each invite a deep connection to nature and the essence of being unencumbered by life's demands.

The raw beauty of Australia's Whitehaven Beach, with its seven kilometers of pure silicate sands, mesmerizes travelers with a visual feast of swirling turquoise waters and heavenly white sandbars. Located in the heart of the Great Barrier Reef, its vibrant marine life and lush rainforests offer a taste of Earth's purest wonders. Each year as the tides shift, the sands change their course, creating beautiful whirls and patterns that are best appreciated from the air.

Across the Pacific, the black sands of Hawaii's Punaluu Beach contrast starkly with the emerald green of coconut palms swaying in the breeze. Here, ancient stories of Hawaiian deities permeate the air, and if you're fortunate, you may witness the spectacle of green sea turtles sunbathing on the shore, embodying the spirit of the island.

For those who've never dipped their toes in the cool embrace of the sea, these journeys inspire not just travel but transformation. It's about finding connection, peace, adventure, and sometimes love, beneath the endless skies.

Great beaches provide not just a destination, but an experience – of meeting new people, tasting the salt of the sea, and watching sunsets that burn across the skies like tales as old as time. They are metaphors for life itself, teaching us to ebb and flow, to embrace what's to come, and to be ever-moving and ever-changed by the tides we encounter. Wanderlust starts its journey at these shorelines, pulling individuals into adventures beyond their dreams and proving life's most beautiful chapters are waiting to be written in the whisper of the waves.

Visiting these beaches is like stepping into a canvas painted by the finest of artists. They're endlessly captivating, reaffirming the idea that some of life's greatest joys require nothing more than a little sand between our toes and the audacious discovery of the next secluded shore. So pack light, let the wanderlust guide you, and remember the best beaches don't just leave sand in your shoes, they leave their mark upon your soul.

How Bays Capture the Heart

There's something undeniably enchanting about a bay, a sentiment that has woven itself through literature and song, beckoning travelers to explore its gentle curves and shimmering waters. The allure of bays lies not just in their tranquil beauty but in the promise of discovery that whispers in the winds that grace their shores. Bays have a way of capturing the heart, offering a balance between the majesty of the ocean and the intimacy of secluded retreats.

Bays are nature's quiet sanctuaries, framed by sweeping headlands that cradle the coast like a protective embrace. These formations are more than geological wonders; they're scenes of natural artistry, created over eons by the patient hands of tides and winds. Each bay has its personality, shaped by the landscape that holds it and the sea that fills it.

Take for instance, the storybook charm of a crescent-shaped bay. Here, the land seems to cradle the water as if in an eternal lullaby, projecting an air of serenity. The gentle curve invites adventurers to find solace and explore the mysteries that lie within. Whether it's the whisper of the trees as they meet the sea breeze or the quiet lap of waves against tender sand, bays beckon the soul to pause and find peace.

The world's bays offer an astounding array of experiences, each promising a unique version of coastal paradise. In the bays of the Pacific Northwest, mist envelopes the water, draping it in an ethereal shroud that hides secrets until the sun breaks through. On a sunlit day, the bays of the Mediterranean sparkle like a gem, their waters an inviting blend of cerulean and turquoise that speak of warmth and adventure.

Venturing into a bay often feels like stepping back in time. Shaded by the cliffside or the canopy of lush forests, the air seems to hum with stories of the past. Imagine standing on the shores of a bay in Greece where the ancient echoes of seafarers still linger, or a secluded inlet in Thailand where time's progress is marked by the rhythm of the tide, not the ticking of a clock.

Bays have long been havens for maritime communities, and across the globe, they're interwoven with the lives of those who call them home. These communities flourish, finding a harmonious balance between the bounty of the sea and the challenges of the open ocean. The bay provides shelter, a calming presence that fosters life and connection, creating a backdrop for stories of resilience, resourcefulness, and amicable coexistence with nature.

The relationship between a bay and its visitors is deeply personal. For some, a bay might invite exploration, drawing them to discover hidden coves accessible only by kayak or to dive beneath the surface and witness the vibrant life below. For others, a bay offers a moment of reflection, where the soft lull of the waves facilitates contemplation and renewal. Here, the mind can wander, untethered from the chaos of the modern world, all within the comforting embrace of the shoreline.

Beneath the water's edge, bays foster rich ecosystems teeming with marine life. These natural harbors feed the soul's curiosity with intricate coral gardens and playful pods of dolphins that make their home in the protective waters. Mangroves and seagrass beds serve as nurseries, nurturing young sea creatures that will one day roam the open ocean.

There's a romanticism tied to bays that touches the heart. Artists and writers often muse about secluded bays, capturing their essence through brushstrokes or poetic verse. The bay's allure lies in the contradiction of its calmness against its untamed natural beauty, a juxtaposition that stirs the soul and inspires creativity. It's easy to see why people return to the bays, both physically and in memory, longing for the stillness found within these curved borders.

Bays also serve as gateways to adventure, offering a starting point for voyages into the unknown. The thrill of setting sail from a sheltered harbor is an age-old story, retold with each new exploration of uncharted waters and discoveries. The pull of adventure resonates within the heart, as bays promise both the safety of return and the excitement of departure.

From the rugged coastlines of New Zealand to the sun-drenched shores of the Caribbean, bays present an invitation to imagine and inspire. They awaken both the dreamer and the adventurer in us, drawing us to explore not just the beauty of the natural world, but the depths of our own hearts. So, let the rhythm of the bays guide you, inviting you to step into their world and discover what has always been right at the heart of their allure.

Chapter 2:
North America's Hidden Treasures

The quieter corners of North America harbor beachside sanctuaries that often slip beneath the radar of mainstream travel guides, yet they possess a beauty that rivals any world-renowned shore. From the jade-hued bays of the Pacific Northwest where misty forests meet crystal waters, to the vibrant Caribbean gems, these locales offer the adventurer and beach lover a treasure trove of unspoiled wonders. Majestic coastal terrains entwine with the whispers of the ocean breeze, turning ordinary moments into timeless memories. Here, travelers seeking solace find respite in secluded coves, where the rhythmic dance of the tide narrates stories of ancient maritime lore, and every sunrise feels like a personal invitation to explore. These hidden gems are not just destinations but invitations to feel the pulse of untouched nature and awaken the wanderlust that lies within every traveler's heart.

Caribbean Gems: Unforgettable Beaches

The Caribbean is synonymous with paradise—a mosaic of islands, each a unique brushstroke on nature's canvas. While many travelers might flock to the well-known shores of Jamaica and the Bahamas, there are hidden wonders that capture the spirit of the undiscovered and offer a slice of solitude amidst the azure expanse.

Picture this: white sand stretching beyond, vanishing into a horizon where sea and sky meld seamlessly. Each island is its own sanctuary, holding secrets that entice the adventurous and leave them

11

longing for more. From the unspoiled beaches of Anguilla to the remote cays of the Turks and Caicos, these jewels of the Caribbean remain tucked away, whispering stories of tranquility and wonder.

Let's embark on a journey to the intoxicating beaches of St. Lucia. Nestled between the lush greenery and dramatic Pitons, the beaches here aren't just sun and sand—they're experiences. Anse Chastanet, with its volcanic silver sands, invites you to explore beneath the water, where vibrant corals tell tales of resilience and beauty. The allure of St. Lucia is not just in lounging by the ocean but in the romance of its untouched beauty, as warm breezes carry the scent of tropical orchids and the gentle rhythms of calypso linger in the air.

Over on Antigua, where "one beach for every day of the year" is a promise not to be broken, the adventure continues. Dickenson Bay is famed for its palm-fringed coastline and luxury resorts, but it's the quieter, lesser-known Rendezvous Bay that beckons those seeking solace. Here, you can find peace under the shade of a swaying palm, the only footprints in the sand your own, as turquoise waters gently lap at the shore.

Then there's the chic appeal of St. Barts, which glitters with French sophistication and Caribbean charm. Hidden beaches like Colombier are accessible only by hiking or by boat, ensuring a secluded haven that feels as exclusive as it does pristine. Peering through the clear, sun-lit water, schools of vibrant fish scatter like jewels across a canvas. It's this simplicity and untouched allure that makes the Caribbean a treasure trove for the discerning traveler.

Let's not forget the enchantment of the Dominican Republic, where the simplicity of Sosúa and the stunning shores of Playa Rincón whisper of tales untold. Playa Rincón, in particular, is a canvas of contrasts—lush mountains give way to strands of silky sand that kiss the sweeping ocean. With a horizon so open and vast, it invites reflection and reprieve from the whirlwind of modern life.

Culebra, a speck of heaven in Puerto Rico's archipelago, offers Flamenco Beach as a marvel of powdery white sands and twinkling blue seas. While many beaches claim to be the best, Flamenco genuinely delivers an unspoiled charm that transports visitors into a vivid postcard scene. Snorkelers and swimmers find joy in its crystal waters, encountering marine life that dances in the sun's rays.

In the Caribbean, time slows, allowing you to enter a world where the corners are softened by sun-kissed memories, and every wave brings a new tale. You can wander to secluded stretches where nature is left to her own devices—a conservation of the wild serenity that defines this part of the world. You'll discover beaches not just as landscapes, but as living, breathing symphonies that invite connection and introspection.

The mere mention of swimming in these pristine waters or strolling along these immaculate sands conjures dreams of wanderers past, of explorations that felt infinite. Somehow, these Caribbean gems have managed to retain that sense of the untouched, offering an invitation to embark on a timeless adventure where each beach becomes a pearl in the necklace of your travels.

Understanding the Caribbean's myriad hidden beaches is an embrace of diversity—each shore providing a different backdrop for romance, exploration, and serenity. The intimate interaction between coral reefs and sandy shores, between secluded coves and expansive vistas, highlights nature's expertise in blending colors, sounds, and sensations to create a paradise like no other.

As you plan your adventure across North America's hidden treasures, let the beaches of the Caribbean be your siren call. Seek out these pockets of calm, where the heart of the ocean beats in harmony with your own. In these Caribbean gems, you'll find not just destinations, but transcendent experiences that resonate long after the sun has set on another perfect day.

Bays of the Pacific Northwest

The Pacific Northwest is a realm where the meeting of land and sea has created an enigmatic tapestry of coastal scenery, often shrouded in mist and mystery. Its many bays stand as sentinels to nature's rugged elegance, each offering its own narrative with every swell and retreat of the tide. It's an area with a reputation for rain and forested landscapes, yet its bays are something of a hidden treasure, rich with the stories of explorers, settlers, and the First Nations that have called these shores home. The allure of these cenic inlets lies not just in the vistas but in the harmonious blend of natural beauty, culture, and history they embody.

Among the first that adventurers might encounter is the iconic Puget Sound, where the salty air mixes with the scent of evergreens. The numerous bays that carve into its coastline, like Elliott Bay or Commencement Bay, are dynamic microcosms of life and commerce, bustling yet tranquil, offering both adventure and refuge. In spring, the Sound's bays often host a symphony of color as wildflowers begin to bloom along the shores. Kayakers and boaters frequent these waters, seeking the chance nocturnal companions beneath starlit skies.

Yet, not all are drawn to this region's pulse of urban life. Those seeking whispers of solitude find it in inlets like Port Townsend Bay or Sequim Bay, which cradle quiet communities where the past is preserved amidst the whispers of the wind. Here, the rhythm of life slows, encouraging reflection as sea breezes and the call of seabirds become an omnipresent lullaby. The surrounding hills and mountains provide a breathtaking backdrop, their forested spines descending abruptly to the watery edge.

The natural world thrives in this corner of the world, supported by a climate that nourishes the land with lushness and fertility. Bays like Willapa Bay and Grays Harbor are testament to this, supporting teeming ecosystems that are vibrant with the dance of wildlife. They are sanctuaries for myriad bird species and the elusive creatures of the deep that occasionally grace the surface with an ethereal presence, creating an ideal setting for nature enthusiasts and photographers alike.

The ambiance of these coastal enclaves changes with the seasons, offering varied yet equally captivating experiences. Summer brings warmth, a gentle sun coaxing picnics on the shorelines and leisurely afternoons in hammocks strung between ancient pines. Autumn turns the landscape into a palette of fiery hues reflected in the glassy waters of bays like Neah Bay, where the transformation is poetry in motion. Even winter, with its grey skies and brisk winds, has a certain charm, wrapping the coast in a cloak of serene isolation.

The cultural narratives of these bays are irrevocably tied to the First Nations and Alaska Native tribes, whose traditions and livelihoods have been intertwined with these waters for millennia. Their presence, past and present, infuses the area with a depth that transcends its natural beauty. Stories passed down through generations linger in the air, echoing the sound of traditional canoes cutting through water, ceremonies conducted on sacred shores, and the everyday life that harmonizes with the rhythm of the tides.

For travelers drawn to explore these remote refuges, the journey is much more than a physical one. Each inlet and sheltered estuary offers its own mystery, inviting introspection and discovery. Like pockets of tranquility in an ever-busy world, the bays of the Pacific Northwest remind visitors of the beauty found in subtlety and the stories whispered by the earth. Exploration here means treading softly and mindfully, for these landscapes are both delicate and majestic, resilient but deserving of our reverence and respect.

As the sun sets, casting its golden glow over the still waters, one can't help but feel a profound connection to these places and their timelessness. The light fades, yet the legacy of these bays—their natural splendor, cultural riches, and awe-inspiring isolation—remains etched in memory. It's a call to return, to rediscover anew, to find solace in their sheltered embrace.

Chapter 3:
The Magic of Central
and South America

In the heart of Central and South America lies a tapestry of coastal enchantment, where the land embraces the sea in a harmony that's nothing short of mesmerizing. Here, the whispers of ancient civilizations linger on the breeze that sweeps across Brazil's enchanted shores and whispers secrets in lush Costa Rican hideaways. Brazil unveils miles of pristine beaches, each with its own unique charm, where the rhythm of samba seems to echo in the crashing waves. Venture into Costa Rica and you'll find secluded getaways where vibrant rainforest kisses the ocean, creating a palette of colors that can't help but captivate the soul. This region is a lush paradise for adventurous spirits and romantics alike, offering not just a journey across stunning landscapes, but a deeper connection with the world's untamed beauty. Whether lounging in a hidden cove or journeying through verdant jungles, the magic of Central and South America beckons you to explore its wonders and find yourself transformed by its awe-inspiring coasts.

Brazil's Enchanted Shores

The rhythm of Brazil is unmistakable—an intoxicating blend of samba beats, lush rainforests, and vibrant cultures. Yet, amidst this lively tapestry, the country's coastline offers a more tranquil symphony that beckons beach lovers and adventurers alike. Brazil's shores are where emerald waves dance with sugar-white sands, where sunrises paint the sky with hues so brilliant that they linger in the soul long after the horizon fades. These enchanting shores are whispers of paradise, inviting explorers to discover their magic.

From the serene bays of Búzios to the sweeping stretches of sand in Jericoacoara, Brazil's beaches are as diverse as they are breathtaking. Each coastal gem tells a story—a unique narrative woven into the larger tapestry of Brazilian culture. Wander the sandy expanses of Praia do Sancho, tucked away on the island paradise of Fernando de Noronha. Consistently ranked among the world's top beaches, its azure waters are teeming with marine life, perfect for snorkeling and diving enthusiasts. It's a place that promises an encounter with nature's grandeur at every turn.

In the south, the island of Santa Catarina captivates with its rugged beauty and lively spirit. Known for its surf-friendly beaches, such as Praia Mole and Joaquina, the island has earned its reputation as a surfer's playground. But beyond the waves, there are secluded coves and hidden hiking trails that reveal panoramic vistas of the Atlantic Ocean. It's a place where adventurers can escape the ordinary and immerse themselves in the calm embrace of nature.

A little further north, the town of Trancoso offers a different flavor of coastal charm. This once-sleepy fishing village has transformed into a chic getaway, famous for its bohemian vibe and stunning beaches like Praia dos Nativos. Here, low-key luxury meets rustic allure; barefoot strolls lead to cliff-top views and quaint squares where artisan crafts enchant visitors. The village's quadrado, a grassy square surrounded by colorful houses, becomes a hive of activity as the sun sets, a testament to Brazil's love for vibrant gatherings.

Venture into Bahia, a region steeped in history and brimming with natural wonders. The beaches of Itacaré, nestled amidst lush Atlantic rainforest, offer a raw, untouched beauty. Coconut groves sway gently in the breeze, framing ribbons of sand that extend as far as the eye can see. This is a havens for eco-conscious travelers, where sustainable initiatives protect the unique ecology and support the local communities. It's a destination that encourages a deeper connection with the Earth and reminds us to tread lightly in paradise.

For those seeking both adventure and solitude, Lençóis Maranhenses National Park is a surreal coastal landscape that defies expectations. It's a realm where vast sand dunes blend seamlessly with turquoise lagoons, creating a dreamscape that shifts with the seasons. Exploring the park is like stepping onto another planet, where the interplay of sand and water forms an ever-changing canvas of beauty. Guided tours by local experts ensure a safe and enriching experience, allowing visitors to learn about the unique ecosystems that thrive in this extraordinary environment.

In Brazil, each beach is a chapter in an endless story, each stretch of sand a canvas painted with tales of explorers and joy seekers. Whether it's lounging on a coconut palm-fringed shore in Paraty or diving into the crystalline waters of Porto de Galinhas, these shores hold a spellbinding power. They offer moments of quiet contemplation and the thrill of discovery, inviting us all to fall under their spell.

Brazil's enchanted coastlines are not just destinations; they are transformational experiences. Here, travelers find not only beauty and adventure but also a sense of belonging. The beaches become more than just places to visit—they become pieces of the heart, destinations to return to both in memory and in journey, time and again.

Secluded Getaways in Costa Rica

In the heart of Central America, Costa Rica beckons with its lush landscapes and pristine beaches. It's a sanctuary for those who seek solace in nature's embrace. This small but mighty country is renowned for its "pura vida" lifestyle—a mindset that celebrates simplicity, freedom, and connection to the earth. You won't find any towering skyscrapers here; instead, the coastline is fringed with jungles rich in biodiversity and beaches that seem to stretch out into infinity.

Costa Rica's Pacific coast is a treasure trove of hidden beaches and secluded bays. The Nicoya Peninsula, for instance, is a world unto itself. Think of long stretches of sand meeting azure waters, where the only sounds are the whispering palm trees and the distant call of exotic birds. Here, you can unplug and unwind, immersing yourself in a place untouched by the clatter of modern life.

Among the jewels of Nicoya, Playa Nosara stands out for its tranquil and picturesque setting. This secluded escape is fringed with lush vegetation, creating the perfect natural barrier to the hustle and bustle of the outside world. It's a mecca for surfers, yogis, and those in search of spiritual rejuvenation. Imagine unwinding with yoga sessions at dawn or catching the perfect wave as the sun sets; it's an experience that feels almost otherworldly.

For the adventurous traveler, the Osa Peninsula offers a slice of untouched paradise. This remote area is famous for Corcovado National Park, a vast protected area teeming with extraordinary wildlife. Venture through dense jungles and hidden waterfalls, witnessing nature in its purest form. The biodiverse waters invite snorkeling enthusiasts to befriend playful dolphins and multi-colored fish, allowing you to explore a vibrant underwater landscape.

Don't miss the opportunity to visit Playa Zancudo, a secret gem nestled on the country's southern Pacific coast. This beach is the epitome of solitude and tranquility, boasting an expansive stretch of soft sand lined with coconut palms. The gentle waves make it an ideal spot for swimming and beachcombing. Here, it feels as if time stands still, providing a perfect backdrop for reflection and relaxation.

Costa Rica's Caribbean side offers its own unique array of secluded getaways. The province of Limón features an idyllic paradise that often goes unnoticed. At Cahuita National Park, travelers are greeted by golden sands and the rhythmic hum of the jungle. This is a place where you can spend hours snorkeling in vibrant coral reefs or simply lounging under the shade of emerald trees.

Punta Uva is another must-visit spot on the Caribbean coast. Often referred to as one of Costa Rica's best-kept secrets, this beach is cherished for its peaceful waters and breathtaking views. The locality encourages harmony between visitors and nature, offering eco-friendly accommodations that complement the area's stunning natural beauty. Whether you're exploring underwater caves or simply savoring a sunset stroll, every moment spent here is steeped in serenity.

One cannot discuss Costa Rica without mentioning its commitment to preserving natural beauty. The country has set aside a quarter of its land for national parks and conservation areas. This dedication ensures that places like Playa Hermosa and Playa Avellanas remain pristine and unspoiled. It's a land where conservation and tourism walk hand in hand, creating a sustainable haven for both nature and visitors alike.

With such a diverse landscape, Costa Rica also offers cultural richness found nowhere else. Alongside the beaches, you'll discover nearby towns and villages that pulse with the rhythm of the local culture. Savor authentic Tico cuisine—think fresh seafood and tropical fruits—and chat with locals who are proud stewards of their corner of paradise.

The choice of whether to explore Costa Rica's Pacific shores or dip into its Caribbean gems is yours, but either path leads to extraordinary experiences and scenes that the soul will cherish long after you've left. These secluded getaways, each a jewel in its own right, perfectly narrate the compelling story of Costa Rica's coastal magic. So as you set foot on this enchanting land, prepare to be spellbound by its natural wonders and infectious spirit of "pura vida."

Chapter 4:
Europe's Coastal Wonders

Nestled along the diverse edges of Europe are coastal wonders that blend history, culture, and raw beauty in a tapestry of unforgettable experiences. From the sun-drenched islands of the Mediterranean, where time drifts as lazily as the clear, azure waves, to the rugged cliffs of Northern Europe, with seas that roar with untamed splendor, every stretch of coastline tells its own story. You'll find charming villages where cobblestone streets lead to hidden coves, and ancient ruins perfectly perched against endless horizons. Here, adventure calls in vibrant hues, whether you're letting the gentle sea breeze guide your wanderings or exploring the nuanced layers of local life. Whether it's the allure of Greece's sunlit shores or the dramatic landscapes of Scandinavia's fjords, Europe's coasts promise enchantment at every turn, inviting you to lose yourself and find a part of yourself all at once.

Mediterranean Dreams: Greece and Beyond

It's the golden glow of a sunset casting its embrace over the Aegean Sea, a kaleidoscope of colors that's virtually impossible to resist. In Greece, each coastline seems to tell its own story, crafted by ancient waves and the whispers of gods. Here, the eternal romance between the land and the sea forms an escape like no other. From the craggy cliffs of Santorini to the serene beaches of Crete, Greece offers a variety of coastal wonders that promise both relaxation and adventure.

When you first set foot on Santorini, it's like stepping into a dream. Those iconic white-washed buildings with their blue domes punctuate the sky, overlooking the azure sea. The beaches here are unique, with sands ranging from volcanic black to bright white, serving as a testament to the island's volcanic origins. While many come to watch the legendary sunsets of Oia, the island's charm lies in the lesser-trodden paths that lead to quiet beaches and secluded coves where you can sit for hours, listening to the gentle waves and pondering life's mysteries.

Yet, beyond Santorini, Greece unfolds a treasure trove of islands and coastal escapes. Mykonos, often synonymous with vibrant nightlife, offers daytime tranquility on its secluded beaches. Elia Beach, one of the longest in Mykonos, provides just the right balance of serene solitude and amenities for a day beneath the sun. And if adventure calls, a boat ride might reveal hidden caves and breathtaking vistas that can only be experienced from the water.

However, Greece's allure doesn't end with its well-known islands. Delving deeper into the Mediterranean, one encounters less frequented gems like Milos, with its dramatic coastline shaped by volcanic activity. Here, Sarakiniko Beach emerges like a surreal moon landscape, with its smooth white rocks contrasting vividly against the deep blue waters. It's a place where geology and imagination seem to conspire to create a stunning visual spectacle.

Crete, the largest Greek island, offers a different kind of enchantment. Its diverse geography allows for sprawling sandy beaches, such as Elafonissi, where pink-hued sands create a blushing shore—a rare natural phenomenon. But Crete's coast is not just about lazing in the sun. The island invites exploration. Hike through the Samaria Gorge and you're rewarded with stunning views that seem to extend to the edge of the earth. The storied beaches of Balos and Falassarna beckon those seeking both adventure and serenity.

Outside of Greece, the Mediterranean continues to weave its tapestry of coastal dreams. Just a short journey away lies Croatia, a land where history and natural beauty intertwine along the Dalmatian Coast. Its coastline, dotted with over a thousand islands, offers endless exploring opportunities. Historic towns like Dubrovnik rise dramatically from the sea, their ancient walls watching over crystal-clear bays. The gentle swells beckon sailors and adventurers alike, blending history with the call of the sea in an irresistible dance.

Across the sea in Italy, the Amalfi Coast presents its own mesmerizing vistas. The cliffs plunge into the Tyrrhenian Sea with an almost reckless beauty, creating a coast that's both rugged and romantic. Towns like Positano and Amalfi cling to the steep cliffs, their pastel hues contrasting against the deep blues and greens of the sea. Every winding road presents a new angle, a fresh perspective of the infinite dance between sea and land, inspiring poets and lovers alike.

Then, travel east to Turkey's Turquoise Coast, and you'll discover an enticing blend of ancient history and coastal splendor. The Lycian Way, a long-distance trail, winds past ruins of civilizations that have long since faded away, yet their presence persists amidst the mountains that cascade into the Mediterranean. It is here where azure waters cradle the coast, each bay a quiet invitation to explore the depths or simply float along the surface, soaking in the beauty and peace.

Reflecting on the Mediterranean, it becomes evident that its true power lies not only in its visual beauty but also in its ability to stir the soul. This region evokes a sense of timelessness, where past and present meet at the water's edge. Whether you're lounging on a secluded beach, navigating the gentle breeze of a sailboat, or simply gazing at the expansive horizon, the Mediterranean assures an experience that remains with you long after you've left its shores.

Ultimately, the Mediterranean isn't just a destination; it's a journey into landscapes where dreams are realized and the spirit finds renewal.

Whether you're drawn by the allure of ancient legends or the promise of unspoiled retreats, these coastal wonders offer an invitation to explore, to dream, and to be inspired by the ever-present dance between land and sea. The journey matters as much as the destination, with each new cove and cliffside offering a fresh perspective and a gentle reminder that the world is full of wonder.

The Untamed Beauty of Northern Europe

Northern Europe's coastlines possess a beauty that is both wild and captivating, resonating with those who seek landscapes unspoiled and rugged. It's a place where nature's raw elements collide in spectacular fashion—where the land meets the sea in a dance of tides against ancient rock formations and expansive fjords. This coastal region whispers the stories of forgotten eras, yet stands timeless and ever-changing, sculpted by the powerful forces of wind and water.

Starting from the windswept isles of Scotland and the awe-inspiring fjords of Norway, these coasts are unlike any other. It's in the craggy cliffs that rise from the ocean, carved rhythmically by centuries of persistent waves, that one might catch a glimpse of the essence of Northern Europe's allure. The roaring of the ocean, combined with the cry of seabirds, creates a symphony that speaks to the heart of adventurers and contemplatives alike, urging them to explore, to linger.

Consider the Scottish Highlands, where rocky shores are interspersed with serene lochs and remote beaches like Luskentyre on the Isle of Harris. Here, white sands and turquoise waters mirror the tranquility found in more tropical locales, but with a solitude that's uniquely northern. The charm lies not just in their beauty, but in their capacity to evoke a sense of melancholy and mystery. Those who wander here often find themselves touched by the profound silence that envelops the landscape, broken only by the occasional rush of wind.

Heading east, the Norwegian coast unveils a tapestry of fjords that stretch deep into the heart of the land. Geirangerfjord and Nærøyfjord, both UNESCO World Heritage sites, are spectacles that inspire awe, with steep cliff faces plunging dramatically into cobalt waters. One can journey through these watery corridors and feel isolated yet connected to the planet in a way that is rare and precious. The fjords' mirror-like surfaces reflect not just the sky, but the soul of the traveler, inviting them into a space of introspection and discovery.

The untamed coast continues to spellbind as you venture toward Sweden and Finland, where archipelagos of verdant islands beckon explorers. In Sweden, the Stockholm archipelago, with its 24,000 islands, forms a labyrinthine paradise for kayakers and sailors alike. Each island has its own character—from rugged and desolate to lush and inviting—creating a string of pearls that dazzles with diversity. It's the kind of place where one can escape into another world, a world far removed from the hustle and bustle of everyday life.

Further north, the Finnish coastline reveals a serene beauty that is equally compelling. The Kvarken Archipelago, also a UNESCO World Heritage site, is known for its unique geological formations. Here, the land is continuously rising from the sea, a phenomenon known as post-glacial rebound, shaping an ever-evolving landscape. Walking along these shores, one can feel the earth's slow and steady breath, a reminder of its ancient rhythms.

Across the Baltic Sea, the coastlines of Estonia and Latvia complete the picture of northern Europe's coastal allure, adding history's weight to the natural elegance. Pärnu, Estonia's summer capital, offers miles of sandy beaches framed by pine forests, while Latvia's Jurmala entices with its charming wooden villas and mineral-rich waters. Both regions promise immersion in nature, alongside a taste of their rich cultural heritage.

It's here, amongst these remote and wind-swept shores, that travelers come not just to witness untamed beauty, but to encounter a profound sense of peace. The landscapes of Northern Europe speak the language of eternity, a dialect best understood in silence and solitude. These coastlines have weathered the eons unchanged, yet they hold the power to change those who wander their lengths.

For those willing to venture beyond the beaten path, Northern Europe's coasts offer a treasure trove of experiences. Wander through quaint fishing villages where time seems to stand still, savor the salty tang of the North Atlantic air, and discover hidden coves that shelter seals and seabirds. Each moment spent exploring this untamed region reveals a new facet of its timeless charm, a call to keep exploring, to keep wandering.

The northern lights often grace these skies, casting an ethereal glow that echoes across the waters, turning the landscape into a wonderland. As those vivid colors dance overhead, the experience is both humbling and enthralling, a perfect reflection of Northern Europe's ineffable allure. In the glow of the aurora, it becomes clear why so many travelers find themselves drawn back to these shores time and again.

Northern Europe's coasts thus stand as a testament to the majesty of nature's power—eternal, unyielding, and breathtakingly beautiful. It's a place where each journey becomes a story, a tapestry woven from the sea's whispers and the land's silent roars. These shores compel us to listen closely, to tread lightly, and to cherish the untamed beauty that defines them.

Chapter 5:
Africa's Serene Shores

Amidst the vibrant tapestry of Africa, the continent's serene shores beckon like a whispered promise at the edge of adventure—a call to those who seek both tranquility and awe-inspiring majesty. From the sun-drenched beaches of the Indian Ocean, where the gentle lap of turquoise waves writes poetry upon sands as fine as sugar, to the mysterious, majestic bays of West Africa, these coastal paradises weave tales of beauty and adventure. As you wander along these shores, the rhythmic dance of ocean and land reveals a world where ancient traditions coexist with untamed nature, offering sanctuary to both weary souls and intrepid explorers. Dive into the azure depths teeming with vibrant marine life, or lose yourself in the soul-stirring sunsets that ignite the sky in a symphony of colors. Here, time seems to drift on the breeze, encouraging you to indulge in the luxury of stillness and reflection that only Africa's coastal wonders can provide.

Beaches of the Indian Ocean

There's something undeniably magical about the Indian Ocean's coastline, where the sun meets sand in a duet of serenity and adventure. The beaches here aren't just slices of paradise; they're symphonies of color and texture that sing to the heart of any traveler. From Seychelles' granite boulders to Madagascar's crimson sands, each spot offers a distinct allure, calling adventurers and romantics alike. But take a closer look, and you'll see that these shores are more than their vistas: they're tapestries of culture and nature, embroidered with stories waiting to unfold.

Starting with the pristine, unspoiled beaches of Seychelles, you find yourself stepping into a world seemingly untouched by time. The islands boast some of the most stunning beaches like Anse Source d'Argent on La Digue Island. Imagine soft white sands offset by towering granite boulders, casting shadows as if playing hide and seek with the sunlight. Here, whether you're snorkeling in crystal-clear waters or walking along the shore, tranquility is your everlasting companion. It's a place where moments stretch and time seems to lose its grip.

Meanwhile, to the south, Madagascar's legendary beaches offer a stark contrast. The famed Nosy Be, known for its pepper plantations and vibrant markets, presents a rhythm of life as vibrant as its coral reefs. Here, the sands aren't just blank canvases but storytelling tapestries interwoven with tales of Malagasy culture and history. The ebb and flow of the tides match the island's heartbeat, inviting surfers to ride azure waves and explorers to discover hidden coves.

Not to be forgotten are Mauritius's coastlines, which are perhaps the most romantic of all. Set amidst lush landscapes, the beaches here seem like they've been cut from a dream. Particularly remarkable is the beach of Île aux Cerfs, where palm trees gently sway in harmony with the ocean breeze, and turquoise waters stretch to meet the azure skies. It's not just a destination; it's the embodiment of a perfect daydream. Couples and families find solace here, united under the canvas of endless horizons and the whispers of gentle waves kissing the shoreline.

For those seeking seclusion, the remote shores of Mozambique offer an unimaginable retreat. With its miles of undisturbed coastline, islands like Bazaruto and Quirimbas present nature in her purest form. Mangroves and coral reefs offer sanctuary to diverse marine life, creating a vibrant underwater world just a snorkel away. Each sunset here is a masterpiece, painted with hues of gold and crimson, reflecting on the tranquil waters as if no dreamer is there to witness it.

Yet, the Indian Ocean beaches are not just for repose. They're gateways to adventure for the bold at heart. Take, for example, Reunion Island, where you can transform from beachcomber to daredevil. Set against dramatic volcanic landscapes, the beaches here aren't just backdrops but thresholds to wild adventures. Paragliding over stately cliffs, surfing off the rugged west coast, or diving into the rich underwater worlds are just a few of the adrenaline-infused invitations that await.

But even as you revel in the diverse offerings, these beaches remind us of the balance between humans and nature. The Tanzanian coast, blessed with beaches like Zanzibar's Nungwi, serves as a living example of sustainable tourism. Here, the balance between preservation and enjoyment is palpable, with eco-friendly lodges offering a model for future beach travel. The vibrant local Swahili culture enriches your stay, as fishermen haul nets at dawn and artisans ply their crafts in sunlit villages.

Emerging from the Indian Ocean is the profound silence of Chole Island in the Mafia Archipelago. Hear the distant call of brooding whales or watch native hawksbill turtles make their journey across the sand. These shores are witnesses to the cycle of life, to beginnings and ends. They affirm that a beach's true essence lies not just in its immediate beauty but in the continuity of experiences it fosters across generations.

In the end, the beaches of the Indian Ocean are a mosaic of life's most cherished elements: beauty, tranquility, culture, and adventure. They serenade the weary soul and challenge the intrepid traveler, offering places where dreams are not just conjured but lived. Wander here, and you'll find that every stretch of sand has its own rhythm, a unique note in a vast melody that flows seamlessly into the ocean's embrace.

The Majestic Bays of West Africa

Picture this: vast horizons where the golden sands meet azure waters, and everything in between is touched by the glow of the African sun. West Africa, an enigmatic blend of cultures, landscapes, and timeless allure, offers bays that may not be household names but possess a grandeur that captivates every traveler's heart. Here, the land and sea waltz together to a rhythm both ancient and new, creating a perfect symphony of serenity and adventure.

Nestled along West Africa's rugged coastline, these bays are destinations of choice for those who seek a departure from the ordinary. One such gem is the Bay of Dakar in Senegal. It's not just a city by the sea, but a vibrant tapestry of art and music that spills onto the shores. The bay offers a unique blend of urban energy and natural beauty, where local fishermen glide alongside pleasure boats, and the notes of a guitar may casually drift your way, carried by a comforting ocean breeze.

Travel further west, and you'll find the tranquil charm of the Freetown Peninsula in Sierra Leone. Surrounded by lush mountains, its bays are secluded retreats where the rainforest sweeps down to the water's edge. Lumley Beach, a crescent-shaped wonder, invites you to dip your toes in its clear waters or simply lounge on the sand with a cold drink in hand, the sun kissing your skin. This coastline boasts magnificent views that even the most eloquent words struggle to capture; it's a place where nature whispers in its own language.

Another hidden marvel lies in Ghana, a country celebrated for its vibrant culture and spirited people. The serene Ada Foah Bay, situated at the estuary of the Volta River, offers diverse experiences from water sports to quiet reflection. The sight of palm trees dancing in the warm breeze is undeniably therapeutic. Here, expect to watch gloriously colorful sunsets that seem to encompass the entire sky, a reminder of the day's soft closure and the quiet promise of tomorrow.

Cape Coast, with its rich history, offers more than just stunning views. Visitors can explore the Cape Coast Castle, a poignant landmark that tells stories of the past even as the waves crash rhythmically against its resilient walls. While the history is somber, the bay itself is a canvas of natural beauty. Wanderers on its shores will find harmony in its vast emptiness, a whisper of the eternal bond between land and sea.

The energetic city of Lagos in Nigeria presents a different coastal experience. Here, the hustle and bustle of one of Africa's largest cities meet the endless stretch of the Atlantic Ocean. The Lagos Lagoon, with its bustling activity, is a contrast to the tranquility found just moments away on Tarkwa Bay. Accessible only by boat, this picturesque spot is a popular retreat for surfers and beachgoers. The rhythm of life in Lagos, a blend of chaos and calm, perfectly mirrors the juxtaposition found at its waters' edge.

Yet, perhaps it's the lesser-known, quieter bays that speak volumes. Hidden along the beaches of Benin is Grand Popo, where the Mono River gently segues into the Atlantic. It's a beach less traveled but teeming with opportunities for exploration. Visitors here might find themselves swept into friendly volleyball games with locals or simply caught in the spell of the bay's unspoiled beauty. The solitude of Grand Popo offers a rare chance to find solace in simplicity and an invitation to explore the authentic side of West Africa.

Each bay across West Africa tells its own story, like beads strung on a shared string, threading a narrative woven with tales of the sea and sky, of human interaction and solitude. The connection between the environment and the communities along these shores is palpable, a synergy that enhances the traveler's experience. It's a reminder that these bays are not just places on a map but vibrant ecosystems, living entities that breathe life into those who pause to appreciate them.

Traveling through West Africa's bays offers a mosaic of experiences, inviting adventure seekers to explore hidden coves and challenging them to embrace the unpredictability of the tides. The bays, with their wild expanses, are a testament to the enduring power and beauty of nature. The air is charged with the calls of seabirds, and the salty tang of the ocean lingers; it's an open invitation to cast off concerns and sink into the present.

Ultimately, the majestic bays of West Africa are more than mere geographical features. They are narratives written in sand and sea, stories of exploration and discovery, resilience and relaxation. They are places that urge us to dream beyond the horizon, where every sunrise heralds new opportunities and every sunset closes the day with quiet grandeur. It's no wonder these coastal treasures become heart-menders, always ready to welcome those who come to their shores with an open heart.

Chapter 6:
Asian Paradises

Asia's coastlines offer a mesmerizing tapestry of landscapes where verdant jungles meet azure seas, promising adventure, serenity, and romance in equal measure. Picture yourself wandering through Thailand's tropical havens, where each beach is a unique escape, painted with golden sands and swaying palms, inviting tranquil introspection as much as thrilling exploration. Further east, the Philippines beckon with islands of solitude, where the world feels delightfully distanced, and time seems to slow its relentless march. The charm of these paradises lies not just in their intrinsic beauty but in their power to rejuvenate weary souls and inspire wanderlust in even the most seasoned travelers. Journeying through these idyllic Asian retreats, you're bound to discover not only exotic landscapes but also hidden facets of yourself, awakened by the vibrant cultures and tranquil seas.

Thailand's Tropical Havens

Thailand's islands are a tapestry of emerald jungles, azure waters, and sun-kissed sands that weave the dream of a tropical haven. Here, nature's palette is at its most enchanting, with hues so vivid that they seem almost imagined. As you set foot on these shores, it becomes abundantly clear why Thailand remains an irresistible lure for beach lovers and adventurers alike. The country's beaches are not merely spots for relaxation but gateways to another world where time takes a backseat, allowing senses to lead the way.

In the bustling heart of the Andaman Sea lies Phuket, Thailand's largest island, often affectionately dubbed "The Pearl of the Andaman." This bustling paradise offers everything from lively nightlife at Patong Beach to the serenity of Laem Singh. Yet, it's not just the beaches that captivate; it's the myriad textures of the island's culture and cuisine. Whether you're hiking to the Big Buddha with panoramic views that stretch beyond the horizon or savoring spicy Tom Yum Goong from a street vendor, every experience is a story unfolding.

The Similan Islands, a national park comprising nine small islands, offer an underwater wonderland. World-renowned among divers, these waters are teeming with vibrant coral reefs and diverse marine life. Snorkelers and divers are greeted by the likes of the majestic manta ray and the elusive whale shark. Above water, the islands invite you to explore their protected white-sand beaches framed by granite boulders, standing like ancient sentinels. Each visit to this archipelago feels like stepping into a living postcard.

Not far from the mainland, the island of Koh Lanta beckons those in search of tranquility. Less crowded than its more famous neighbors, Koh Lanta's beaches like Klong Dao and Kantiang Bay offer an idyll of golden sands and azure waters. But perhaps its greatest appeal is the neighboring Mu Ko Lanta National Park, where verdant jungles and hidden waterfalls promise adventures for those who wander off the beaten path.

The Koh Phi Phi archipelago encapsulates the quintessential beauty so often depicted in travel brochures. Koh Phi Phi Leh's Maya Bay gained fame as the backdrop for the film "The Beach," and its striking limestone cliffs and crystal-clear waters continue to draw in visitors. Yet, while it may boast cinematic fame, the island unfolds quieter corners too, where time slows down and nature's whispers can be heard. It's these hidden facets that reveal the real magic of a place caressed by the tides.

Further along the Andaman coast, the island of Koh Kradan might be lesser-known, but it's no less mesmerizing. Here, an unspoiled charm awaits, perfect for those in search of peaceful retreat. There's an intimacy with nature on this island, where the gentle lapping of waves and the rustle of palm fronds form the soundtrack of your stay. Snorkeling reveals some of the best underwater vistas in the Trang province, with reefs located just a few meters from the shore.

On the other side of the Thai peninsula, the Gulf of Thailand unveils a different kind of allure. Koh Samui, known for its boutique resorts and vibrant nightlife, offers a mix of luxury and authentic Thai experiences. Beneath the coastal chic vibe lies a thriving community of artisans, whose markets provide a sensory delight of colors, scents, and tastes. Each village tells a story, from the daily catch of fishermen to the bustling life of the markets.

Nearby, Koh Phangan intrigues with its contrasting faces. Known globally for its full moon parties that light up Haad Rin, Koh Phangan also offers more serene retreats. Some of its northern beaches, like Bottle Beach and Thong Nai Pan, are hidden treasures ensconced within lush jungles. Trekking to these remote beaches is part of their allure, requiring a journey through dense greenery that heightens the sense of discovery upon arrival.

Koh Tao, or Turtle Island, is a haven for diving enthusiasts. Almost every beach is a starting point for underwater exploration, with dive sites that range from beginner-friendly bays to advanced underwater landscapes like Chumphon Pinnacle. Above the waves, the island maintains a laid-back charm with panoramic views from the Mae Haad hills and sunsets best enjoyed with a chilled coconut in hand.

These islands are more than just destinations; they are realms where every footprint changes the landscape of exploration, where every wave that kisses the shore brings a secret from the deep. Inviting as they are beautiful, Thailand's tropical havens are places to fall in love with the concept of paradise itself. For those looking to lose themselves and find a deeper connection with the world, these islands offer not just an escape, but a beckoning promise of timeless adventure.

The Philippines: Islands of Solitude

Tucked away in the expanse of the Pacific, the Philippines beckons with its promise of solitude and untouched beauty. In a country composed of over 7,000 islands, each offers its own slice of paradise—a haven for those looking to escape the busyness of modern life. Imagine finding a place where time slows, and your only priority is to listen to the gentle lap of waves on pristine shores. This is the magic that envelopes the Philippine archipelago, where islands serve as sanctuaries for the soul.

Take for instance Palawan, a name synonymous with unspoiled natural beauty. It's often highlighted as the crown jewel among the Philippine islands. Here, the azure waters blend seamlessly with the limestone karsts that jut imposingly from the ocean. El Nido and Coron, popular Palawan destinations, might attract more visitors, but there's still plenty of undiscovered coastline where solitude reigns supreme. Small, secluded beaches are just a boat ride away, each a testament to the timelessness of nature's artistry.

Every adventure in the Philippines is as rich in culture as it is in natural beauty. On the island of Siargao, known primarily as a surfer's paradise, you'll find more than just waves. The island's landscapes offer crystal-clear lagoons and hidden caves waiting to be explored. Exploration here is not just a journey through nature but also a deep dive into the warm and welcoming spirit of the Filipino communities, who often share their ways of life with travelers seeking authenticity.

Venture to Mindanao's lesser-known islands, and you might feel like an explorer discovering a new world. Camiguin, a tiny island province, packs a punch with a landscape dotted with volcanoes, waterfalls, and hot springs. Each corner of the island tells a story, and it's easy to feel like you've stepped into another time and place, where the only thing interrupting your solitude is the hum of the cicadas.

The Philippines' isolation doesn't mean a lack of adventure. For those with a spirit for exploration, the Bacuit Archipelago offers a labyrinth of islands, each with its own charm. Hidden lagoons and secret beaches await those willing to paddle kayak or hop on a local banca boat. The sea is a canvas here, painted with endless shades of blue and green, a stark contrast to the karst cliffs that stand watch over these secluded waters.

Sometimes, solitude comes from being one with the ocean itself. Diving enthusiasts often cite the Tubbataha Reefs Natural Park, a UNESCO World Heritage Site, as a must-visit. Here, the underwater world rivals any story of solitude above, offering a serene escape beneath the waves. Vibrant corals, schools of fish, and gentle giants like whale sharks join you in this underwater sanctuary, reminding you of the ocean's wonders that continue beyond the horizon.

Even islands like Cebu, noted for their bustling metropolis, offer a slice of tranquility. Offshore, the serene beauty of Bantayan Island invites visitors to lazy days spent lounging on white sands, only occasionally pausing to float in calm, translucent waters. The island life encourages a slow pace, letting travel enthusiasts soak in the moment and leave the rush of urban living far behind.

The Philippine's islands of solitude are also envelopes of romance. Batanes, famed for its rugged landscapes and quaint stone houses, provides a backdrop where intimacy seems a natural consequence of its beauty. Lush rolling hills dotted with cattle and welcoming lighthouses echo stories of bygone eras. Here, you'll find spaces perfect for reflection and connection—both with nature and loved ones.

As you travel through these islands, you'll notice that the joy doesn't just lie in the landscapes but within the people who inhabit these lands. Filipinos are known for their hospitality and warmth, offering a friendly smile or guidance to a hidden waterfall with the same ease. The connections made here are as lasting as the sunsets that paint the night skies a myriad of colors.

For the adventurer craving guidance in the art of true retreat, the Philippines presents itself as a master in solitude—a place where one can find both adventure and peace. With miles of untainted coastline and a tapestry of cultural richness, these islands whisper promises of adventure yet to be taken. The Philippines stands not just as a destination but as a testament to the tranquility the world still harbors.

Whether seeking the thrill of new horizons or the comfort of serene beaches, the Philippines offers a palette of experiences designed to soothe and inspire. Step into this archipelago, and you step into a world where time floats alongside the clouds; a promise of solitude in an otherwise bustling world. Such is the allure of the Philippines—reminding us that sometimes, the most profound journeys begin with a touch of solitude.

Chapter 7:
Australasia's Coastal Beauty

Australasia is a realm where nature's splendor unfolds along the shores, offering breathtaking landscapes that romance the adventurer's soul. Australia, with its sun-kissed coastline, boasts legendary beaches from the iconic Bondi to the secluded stretches of Whitehaven, where pristine sands and azure waters create a tableau of serene beauty. Here, each wave whispers tales of centuries past, inviting you to unwind and explore the vivid marine life beneath the surface. Venturing southeast, New Zealand's tranquil bays offer a different kind of magic; a sense of timeless peace pervades places like the Bay of Islands, where lush hills cascade to meet the sea in a gentle embrace. Whether it's the adventurous surfer conquering vast swells or the contemplative traveler marveling at a sunset's painted sky, Australasia's coasts captivate with a promise of unforgettable experiences and the profound realization that sometimes, paradise is a place you stand in.

Australia's Legendary Beaches

Australia, a land of vast horizons and endless skies, offers a coastal bounty that beguiles the senses and awakens the spirit of adventure. Its beaches are not just stretches of sand meeting the sea but are an integral part of the country's cultural fabric and natural beauty. From the pristine shores of the Whitsunday Islands to the rugged cliffs of the Great Ocean Road, Australia's beaches provide a diverse tapestry of experiences for travelers seeking both solace and exhilaration.

Imagine standing on Whitehaven Beach, located on Whitsunday Island. Often hailed as the pinnacle of beach perfection, its sand is nearly pure silica, resulting in a powdery white expanse that starkly contrasts the vivid turquoise sea. As your toes sink into the soft sand, you're enveloped by natural silence, save for the gentle melody of waves lapping at the shore. This beach isn't just a feast for the eyes; it's an escape into serenity, a place where time has a way of pausing ever so slightly, allowing you to savor each tranquil moment.

Then there's the Gold Coast, where the sands pulse with energy and life. Known both for its long stretches of sandy heaven and its iconic surf breaks, the Gold Coast is a paradise for surfers and sunbathers alike. You'll find bustling beach towns offering endless entertainment options, from trendy cafes to vibrant nightlife. But just around the corner, hidden gems like Burleigh Heads provide a quieter, more reflective space, where the waves roll in with an almost meditative rhythm perfect for morning yoga or an evening stroll.

Venturing further south, the allure of the Great Ocean Road beckons. Here, the untamed beauty of Bells Beach calls to the intrepid surfer with its powerful swells and legendary surf competitions. For others, the rugged cliffs and the famous Twelve Apostles, majestically rising from the Southern Ocean, offer a breathtaking vista that inspires feelings of insignificance and wonder at nature's grandeur.

The magic of Australia's beaches also lies in their seclusion. Cable Beach in Western Australia, with its endless expanse of golden sand, creates a canvas that sunsets paint each evening in fiery hues. It's a place where you can truly feel the edge of the world, ride a camel along the shore, or simply sit back and enjoy the symphony of colors that fill the sky.

Heading north, explore the remote and beautiful Cape Tribulation in the Daintree Rainforest. Here, the Daintree meets the sea—a lush and ancient forest kissing the coastline, blending two vibrant ecosystems. It's a convergence that feels almost primordial, where the rainforest hums with life and the ocean whispers stories of the past. The beaches here are quiet, untamed, and oh so beautiful, offering an experience that feels like stepping into another world.

Australia doesn't only offer iconic visual landscapes but also an immersive cultural experience. The beaches serve as gateways to understanding the country's indigenous heritage. Sacred spaces dot the coastline, long held by indigenous Australians who have stories tied to every rock and wave. Taking part in cultural tours allows you to glean insights into traditions and histories that have flourished beside these waters for tens of thousands of years.

And who could forget the coral-fringed beaches of Ningaloo Reef, where the chance to swim with whale sharks draws adventurous souls from around the globe? Snorkeling or diving here feels like entering a dream world teeming with colorful marine life and vibrant coral gardens. Each dive reveals new wonders and unlocks secrets of the ocean that leave an indelible mark on those lucky enough to experience it.

Australia's beaches are more than mere destinations—they're experiences that touch the soul. They offer escape, adventure, romance, and discovery, all under the sun-kissed skies of this extraordinary continent. Whether you're riding the perfect wave, exploring subaqueous wonders, or simply reveling in the sound of the surf and warming sun, each beach tells its own tale of beauty and mystery, waiting just for you.

New Zealand's Tranquil Bays

In the heart of the Southern Hemisphere, New Zealand offers a coastline that rivals any in the world for beauty and peacefulness. Scattered along its shores are bays, each more enchanting than the last. With stretching beaches and secluded coves framed by rugged cliffs and lush vegetation, these bays whisper the promise of serenity. New Zealand's tranquil bays are not just destinations; they're experiences, waiting to envelop travelers in their calming embrace.

Imagine standing on the sands of Cathedral Cove, where the surf gently kisses the shore as limestone formations rise dramatically from the water. This bay offers a glimpse of untouched beauty that feels almost like a secret the Earth has been guarding for centuries. Accessible by a coastal walk through native bush, Cathedral Cove invites explorers to take their time, breathing in the salty air and feeling the world's edges soften. It's a place where time slows down and the hum of life pauses at the gate of nature's cathedral.

Further north, Oneroa Bay on Waiheke Island offers a different kind of allure, blending seclusion with a hint of the cosmopolitan. Fringed by boutique vineyards and olive groves, this bay embodies a laid-back sophistication. The turquoise waters call to those who yearn for gentle adventures or lazy days pleasures—whether it's paddling a kayak across the gentle waves or simply sunbathing under the gracious New Zealand sun. Here, sweet island life harmonizes with a touch of elegance, creating an unforgettable setting for romance or reflection.

Let us drift to the South Island, where the majestic curve of the Abel Tasman coastline reveals a string of bays as if painted by an artist's loving hand. Tonga Bay captivates with its golden sands and rich, emerald waters. It's the kind of place that encourages exploration on foot or by sea, where trails weave through verdant forests before spilling out onto hidden sands, and kayaking routes chart paths through waters teeming with playful seals and gliding stingrays. These bays, wrapped in national park protections, offer sanctuaries for both wildlife and human wanderers alike.

Venture to Milford Sound, a fjord that's often cloaked in mist, adding to its mystical atmosphere. Iconic Mitre Peak mirrors in the calm waters of Harrison Cove, crafting a scene of sheer vertical cliffs meeting the sea—a cathedral built by nature herself. This bay, carved by ancient glaciers and echoing with the songs of cascading waterfalls, urges visitors to surrender to sublime wonder. A cruise through these inky depths or a paddle along its edges is a journey into a world that feels primordial and eternal.

Tucked into the Bay of Islands, Opua Bay charms with its pockets of peace amidst a backdrop of historical intrigue and maritime zest. A gateway to a sailor's paradise, the bay teems with yachts seeking both adventure and solace. Once a harbor for whalers and traders, Opua invites the curious to dig into its past, to explore the quaint towns and learn of the first encounters between Māori and European settlers. This bay echoes with stories carried by the winds, waiting for intrepid listeners.

Nowhere else does nature paint with such a rich, varied palette as on New Zealand's Coromandel Peninsula. At Otama Bay, the canvas of white sands and azure seas is bordered by dunes whispering in the breeze, the whole scene backed by rolling hills. Hidden away from the rush of busier locales, Otama is a retreat for those who dream of the simple pleasures: long walks, lengthy reads, and late-day reflections as the sun dips below the horizon.

The journey through New Zealand's tranquil bays isn't complete without a nod to the cultural depths they harbor. Each bay is a reflection of the Māori heritage that permeates the land and seascape. From the legends of Kupe to the sacred significance of natural landmarks, the cultural threads running through these bays are as vital as the ecological ones. Paua shells dotting the sands are not just treasures of color and shimmer; they're symbolic of life and fertility, connecting every visitor to a deeper narrative of identity and belonging.

And so, for the traveler who dreams of places where the world is less loud and more profound, New Zealand's bays offer an unparalleled embrace. Each bay is more than a destination; it's an invitation to rediscover balance—between adventure and rest, between reflection and revelation. Here, the tides carry away the weight of the restless world, leaving the spirit light, renewed, and free to wander on paths less traveled. Truly, the tranquil bays of New Zealand aren't just places on a map; they're passages to tranquility, waiting to be discovered again and again.

Chapter 8:
Middle Eastern Mystique

In the heart of the Middle East, where the desert meets the azure waves, an enigmatic allure takes shape along the shores of Oman and the hidden bays of the Red Sea. Here, ancient myths blend seamlessly with the rhythmic dance of tides, creating a unique coastal experience that beckons the adventurous and the romantic alike. The rugged cliffs and golden sands of Oman's coastline whisper tales of sailors and traders who once navigated these waters, while secluded inlets of the Red Sea harbor unparalleled marine diversity, waiting to thrill divers and explorers. The serenity found amidst these mystical landscapes is not just a retreat from the chaos of everyday life; it's a journey into a realm where the vastness of nature promises both reflection and inspiration. As you trace these shores, the Middle Eastern mystique unfolds like a tapestry woven with stories of old, where every beach and bay holds a secret longing to be discovered.

The Unique Shores of Oman

Nestled along the southeastern coast of the Arabian Peninsula, Oman offers an array of enchanting shores that are as diverse as the tales of ancient mariners who once roamed its seas. Oman's beaches are a blend of rugged beauty and serene escapades, inviting adventurers and sunseekers alike to experience a different facet of the Middle East. Unlike the glossy high-rises and bustling attractions of its neighboring countries, Oman presents a country where the coastline is a tapestry woven with history, nature, and undisturbed charm.

From the stretching sands of Salalah to the turquoise waters hugging Muscat, Oman's shores are a testament to nature's splendor. Salalah, particularly during the Khareef season, transforms into a lush green wonderland; the monsoon rains create a landscape filled with waterfalls and vibrant greenery. The beaches here are perfect for those who revel in the solitude of unspoiled nature, where the sound of the waves is a constant companion, and the only footprints you might encounter are your own.

In contrasts as striking as its hinterland deserts, the coastline of Musandam showcases dramatic fjords—often called the "Norway of Arabia." These narrow inlets, known locally as "khors," are accessible only by dhow, a traditional wooden boat, and offer a mesmerizing dance of azure waters against limestone cliffs. Cruising through these waters, time seems to stand still, presenting a perfect opportunity for reflection and an escape from the clamor of modern life.

Venturing slightly off the beaten path, the coasts of Ras Madrakah present untamed beauty where stark desert landscapes meet the rushing waves of the Indian Ocean. The beaches here are not just about the sea; they are lands of intricate rock formations crafted by time and tide, where adventurers can discover hidden inlets and watch sea turtles lay their eggs on the sandy shores. There's a sense of discovery around each corner, and the culture of the local fishing villages adds a rich tapestry of stories and traditions to be uncovered.

Oman's unique shores are steeped in history, much of which intertwines with the ancient Silk Road. The historic coastal city of Sur is a testament to this. Known for its shipbuilding heritage, Sur is where traditional dhows are crafted, echoing the region's maritime legacy. Walking along its beaches, one can imagine the bustling days of old when merchants traded spices and goods, leaving a mosaic of cultures and stories behind. Today, the tranquility of Sur's beaches is interrupted only by the gentle hum of the ocean and occasional laughter of local families enjoying a day in the sun.

Exploring the beaches of Oman isn't just about soaking in the sublime scenery; it's about embracing an adventure filled with elements of surprise. Each visit promises a different experience, as no two days are alike under Oman's sun-kissed skies. At Bandar Jissah, divers and snorkelers are treated to an underwater paradise where vibrant coral reefs play host to an array of marine life. Here, the water seems to shimmer with distinctive hues, unveiling a colorful underwater spectacle that promises to enthrall even seasoned ocean lovers.

In Oman's north lies Al Haffa, a pristine stretch of sandy beach fringed by coconut palms. The allure of this coconut-studded coastline is its simplicity, where gentle waves lap against your feet as the aroma of frankincense drifts from nearby souks. Unlike the crowded beaches many travelers might be accustomed to, Al Haffa retains a peacefulness that becomes a balm for the soul, encouraging moments of meditation and introspection.

No account of Oman's beaches would be complete without a nod to the majestic Ras al Jinz. This protected reserve is one of the most important nesting grounds for the endangered green turtle. Arriving before dawn, visitors can witness the awe-inspiring sight of turtle hatchlings making their first pilgrimage towards the sea—a perfect metaphor for the journey of discovery that awaits anyone willing to explore Oman's coastline.

Oman's beauty is deeply tied to its people, whose warm hospitality stands as one of its greatest charms. The ubiquitous cups of spiced tea offered by locals are more than a refreshment; they are an invitation to learn more about their lives, their stories, and the land they cherish. Engaging with Oman's hospitable inhabitants presents an authentic experience of not just its beaches, but its culture as well, enriching any traveler's road of discovery.

In conclusion, the unique shores of Oman invite those who seek not just a beach but a narrative; an adventure that offers more than the typical postcard scenery. Each beach tells a story, woven into the ocean's rhythms and the sands of time. For those willing to wander its coasts, Oman promises a mystical escape echoing with endless tales of the desert meeting the sea. Here, travelers find a perfect blend of adventure, tranquility, and romance—a true embodiment of the Middle Eastern mystique.

Hidden Bays of the Red Sea

The Red Sea, a shimmering ribbon separating Africa from the Arabian Peninsula, holds secrets in its azure embrace—secrets that invite the weary traveler to pause, ponder, and plunge into its beckoning depths. Imagine bays steeped in myths and stories, landscapes sculpted by time and tides, and waters that dance between tones of teal and deep sapphire. The allure of the Red Sea is magnetic, drawing those who seek both solitude and connection with the vastness of nature.

The shores of the Red Sea are where desert meets the ocean, painting a palette of contrasts. The sun-drenched sands seem to stretch eternally, whispering of ancient caravans and endless journeys. Here, in the embrace of hidden bays, it is easy to find echoes of the past mingling with the soothing rhythm of waves kissing the shore.

It's these secluded bays, untouched by the crowds of mainstream tourism, that promise a kind of adventure that speaks to the soul. The journey begins long before you cast your sail or slip beneath the waves. The roads leading to these hidden gems often meander through stark desert landscapes, where solitude is broken only by the occasional whisper of wind over the sand dunes. This is the approach to Berenice, a bay that holds its mysteries as securely as the sands.

Berenice is one such desert jewel where the past meets the present. Once a bustling port in ancient times, today it offers a sanctuary for those seeking tranquility. Its waters teem with marine life, lend themselves to thrilling underwater exploration. Snorkeling here reveals vibrant coral gardens, teeming with the aquatic ballet of angelfish and parrotfish. A dive unveils the secrets of submerged shipwrecks, each with tales etched in rust and coral that evoke the romance of a bygone era.

Then there is Ras Banas, a bay that sleeps between legends and reality. Tucked away where the desert gently whispers to the sea, it offers a seclusion that is both rare and enchanting. At Ras Banas, the sunsets paint the sky in hues of orange and purple, creating a canvas that invites reflection. The beauty here is stark yet undeniably poetic, speaking to the traveler who yearns for connection but revels in isolation.

Yet, it is the bay of Marsa Alam that captivates many with its promise of untouched beauty. A relatively new discovery to international travelers, Marsa Alam remains a hidden paradise waiting to unfold its secrets. Its clear waters, a mirror to the sky, cradles some of the most vibrant coral reefs you will find anywhere on the planet. Here, adventurous souls can dive into an underwater wonderland where time stands still.

The shores of the Red Sea are steeped in stories as old as time, where the ebb and flow offer a soundtrack to tales of mermaids and mariners. Exploring these hidden bays is an invitation to witness history resting just beneath the surface. The guardians of these secrets, small fishing villages, dot the coastline like pearls on a strand. They offer hospitality that feels as timeless as the sea itself, with people who have learned to live in harmony with the ocean's changing moods.

But not all the marvel of the Red Sea lies beneath the waves. As the sun sets, the coastal skies come alive, stars winking into view in the vast tapestry above. It's a celestial show free from the polluting lights of cities, where constellations guide the imagination, and moonlight paints the seascape in silver.

The hidden bays of the Red Sea promise more than solitude—they offer a rejuvenating communion with nature that words can scarcely capture. Each bay, with its unique beauty and cultural lore, invites introspection. It provides a space to escape the humdrum of daily life and rediscover the thrill of adventure and the wonder of discovery.

For the adventurous traveler, the journey to these coastal paradises doesn't end when you step onto the plane home; it leaves an indelible mark on the heart. The Red Sea's hidden bays are a call to storytellers and dreamers alike, birthing tales of wistful days spent wandering its shores, breathing in the salt-kissed air.

These quiet crescents of sand and sea, offering solitude and splendor, are waiting for those with a yearning for the sublime. As travelers seeking the exceptional, we are reminded that the real treasures of the Red Sea are not merely its vibrant aqualife or sunsoaked beaches—but the echoes of history interwoven with the stillness of today, inviting each of us to become a piece of the sea's endless narrative.

Chapter 9:
Caribbean Delights

As we drift into the hypnotic embrace of the Caribbean, we're met with an unmatched palette of turquoise waters and sun-kissed beaches, each more enchanting than the last. Imagine the allure of the Lesser-Known Islands, where secret stretches of sand beckon the weary soul searching for quietude. These gems, untouched by the frenzy of mass tourism, provide a canvas for spontaneous adventure and serene reflection. Meanwhile, the Greater Antilles boast hidden coves that hold stories of pirates and explorers, inviting modern-day travelers to uncover their mysteries. It's a realm where time slows, and the rhythm of the tide becomes the soundtrack to your wanderlust-driven journey. In this paradise, every sunset feels like a brushstroke of magic, painting the sky in hues that ignite the heart's deepest desires for exploration and wonder.

Beaches of the Lesser-Known Islands

The Caribbean is a symphony of turquoise waters and lush foliage, with each island playing its unique note. Beyond the well-trodden paths of the popular destinations, there lies a collection of lesser-known islands, each with its own hidden beaches just waiting to be unveiled. These spots aren't just places on a map; they're sanctuaries for those seeking solitude and raw natural beauty. The roads may be less traveled, but the rewards are endlessly enriching.

Take Isla de Culebra, for example. Nestled within the Spanish Virgin Islands, it boasts Flamenco Beach—an expanse of pearly sand fringed by palm trees, perfect for those moments when the hustle of life feels overwhelming. Snorkeling here isn't just an activity; it's a dance with vibrant corals and darting fish, each interaction serving as a gentle reminder of the underwater world's magic. It's a place where time's lost hold can be keenly felt, where every minute is a blessing, every hour a poem.

Over on Dominica, the "Nature Island," you'll find black sand treasure troves like Batibou Beach. These shores, forged from the island's volcanic past, are nothing short of mesmerizing. With every wave that kisses the shore, there's a whisper of ancient stories layered within the grains of sand. Whether you're stretched out under a canopy of lush forest or taking a leisurely swim, Batibou offers a sense of being cradled by the island itself.

St. Vincent and the Grenadines invite explorers to discover gems like Lower Bay Beach on Bequia. Diving headfirst into the crystal clear water here, you're met with an array of underwater life that paints a vivid portrait against the sun-drenched backdrop. Decked out with charming beach bars that echo the laid-back atmosphere, Lower Bay is an invitation to unwind, to indulge in good company and laughter with the locals, and to forge bonds beyond borders.

If you find yourself in the British Virgin Islands, Anegada's Loblolly Bay will captivate you. Unlike its mountainous neighbors, Anegada is flat—a coral atoll that offers a dazzling array of secluded beaches. Loblolly Bay stands out for its untouched beauty, a sanctuary sculpted by nature itself. Here, each sunrise and sunset is an art show, with colors so vibrant they're almost unreal, sweeping over the bay like a soft embrace.

Meanwhile in Saba, the aptly named "Unspoiled Queen," there's a rugged elegance to its shores. With limited sandy stretches, spots like

Well's Bay offer a picturesque blend of cliffs and hidden nooks where adventurers can find solace. The allure of Saba isn't just in the landscape but in its hiking trails that lead to panoramic vistas, compelling visitors to see the island's challenges as gateways to hidden joys.

Over on the tranquil shores of Grenada's Carriacou, the sands of Paradise Beach truly live up to their name. Here, tranquility isn't an aspiration; it's a reality. As you lounge on this slice of paradise, you may find yourself reflecting on the delicate jewel of life's simpler pleasures. With the sea's rhythmic lapping and the warm breeze fluttering through swaying palms, you'll be transported to a state of serene contentment.

In the south, off the coast of Venezuela, the archipelago of Los Roques promises a vision of sugar-white sands and azure waters that seamlessly blend into a realm of solitude and beauty. Here, on islands like Crasqui, the draw isn't the hustle of resort life but the gentle drift of a kayak on calm lagoons or the quiet connections made with feathered visitors in this birdwatcher's paradise.

Journeying to Anguilla, the beach of Savanna Bay offers more than its fair share of postcard-perfect beauty. With its powdery sands flanked by a wide-open sea, it's a place where ambitions seem to pause and musings flourish. Savanna Bay is an artist's palette, a storyteller's haven, an adventurer's promise. It calls to you with the lure of what could be, urging a dive into both its waters and the depths of your own imagination.

On the less known shores of Montserrat, a silver lining emerges amid the volcanic ash: Rendezvous Beach. It stands as a symbol of resilience and renewal. Quiet and isolated, it becomes a stage set for introspection and dreams. Here, you'll find that even in isolation, there's a profound connection—be it the ethereal bond to nature or a reconnection with yourself.

The Caribbean's lesser-known islands are a treasure map etched with secrets waiting to be uncovered. Their beaches are more than destinations; they're canvas and cocoon, explorer and oracle. These serene stretches of sand invite you to step away from the ordinary and peer into a world where nature reigns supreme, bows to no one, and offers tranquility in the cadence of its tides. To visit these hidden gems is to embrace a travel experience that's profoundly human, and exceptionally extraordinary.

Secret Coves of the Greater Antilles

In the heart of the Caribbean, where azure meets sand in a swirl of intoxicating beauty, lie the secret coves of the Greater Antilles. These hidden pieces of paradise, tucked away from the bustling crowds, offer a unique blend of tranquility and adventure, promising an escape into a world that feels otherworldly. As you embark on a journey through these secluded havens, you'll find it's not just about the pristine beaches and crystal-clear waters; it's about the stories whispered by the winds and waves, the cultural tapestry that ties together land and sea.

The mesmerizing island of Jamaica hosts a myriad of these secret coves. Take a journey to Frenchman's Cove, a spot that merges elegance with untamed nature. Here, a river gently meanders into the ocean, offering a unique experience of fresh and saltwater. As you step into this tranquil cove, you're enveloped by a lush canopy, the songs of tropical birds your only company. It's a place where time seems to stand still, offering the perfect setting for contemplation or an invigorating swim beneath the warm Caribbean sun.

In Puerto Rico, the hidden gem of Playa Buyé beckons with its golden sands and gentle waves. This isolated slice of heaven is a favorite among locals—an endorsement in itself. As you walk along the postcard-perfect coastline, the vibrant culture of Puerto Rico becomes palpable. Stop by a local kiosko to savor freshly prepared seafood, or simply sip on a cool coconut while watching the sun dip lazily into the sea. The peacefulness of Playa Buyé invites introspection, making it an ideal retreat for those looking to unwind and connect with nature.

Cuba, with its rich history and vibrant culture, unfolds another layer of Caribbean magic. Cayo Jutías, an often-overlooked stretch of white sandy beaches on the northwestern coast, is a place of wild and unspoiled beauty. Here, you can paddle through mangrove channels or laze beneath the docile shade of casuarina trees. As you explore the winding paths of this secluded island, the rhythmic sounds of salsa echo in the distance, beckoning you to join in its vibrant embrace.

Hispaniola, the island shared by the Dominican Republic and Haiti, offers its own collection of secretive nooks. In the Dominican Republic, Playa Frontón awaits intrepid explorers willing to undertake the scenic trek or boat ride to reach it. This hidden paradise, shielded by towering limestone cliffs, offers a spectacular setting for snorkeling and diving. Vibrant coral gardens and an array of marine life lie beneath its cerulean waters, inviting underwater adventurers to discover an aquatic wonderland.

Meanwhile, Haiti, with its rich folkloric traditions, reveals pockets of serenity like Jacmel Beach. Known for its artistic community and festive celebrations, Jacmel offers a unique experience that combines cultural immersion with coastal relaxation. Wander through its cobblestone streets and observe the local artisans at work before heading to the less-traveled beach, where you can sit back and watch the unhurried life of the bay village unfold.

Venturing farther into the archipelago, the island of Saint Thomas in the U.S. Virgin Islands presents the intimate Magens Bay. Renowned for its sheltered waters, this cove offers an ideal blend of accessibility and seclusion. Early morning visits promise the solitude of a freshly painted sunrise, while the bay's calm waters invite a range of activities from leisurely kayaking to snorkeling with the marine life that thrives within its gentle, protective grasp. The surrounding hills, blanketed in emerald hues, provide mesmerizing vantage points across the bay.

These secret coves are more than breathtaking destinations; they are testimonials of nature's ability to enchant and heal. Each cove has its personality and charms, enticing travelers with tales of pirates, hidden treasures, or the simple promise of peace. They're places where every grain of sand has a story to tell, every breeze carries the scent of adventure, and every sunset promises a moment of unparalleled divine beauty.

To journey through the Greater Antilles is to indulge in a symphony of sights, sounds, and sensations. The ocean's gentle lullaby, the vibrant hues of the horizon, the whispers of the wind mingling with the rustle of the palms—each element contributes to an unforgettable experience. Pioneering through lesser-known paths and finding your secluded sanctuary is a testament to the enduring allure of these hidden gems. As you explore these coasts, you'll carry away memories imprinted through sunlit strolls and moonlit reflections, reminders of a time when the world was yours to discover, one secret cove at a time.

Chapter 10:
Polynesian Pearls

Imagine a horizon where turquoise waters gently brush against the soft, white sands of French Polynesia, a place where time seemingly pauses to let you bask in nature's romance. Here, the sky feels closer, the sun warmer, and every evening the sunset paints the heavens with hues impossible to capture elsewhere. These jewels of the South Pacific promise not just a vacation, but a voyage into serenity and wonder. Remote retreats await, tucked away on distant shores where the world is silent save for the soothing lullaby of waves. Each island tells its own love story—between sea and sand, man and nature. As you wander these sacred atolls, you discover peace layered with adventure, allowing the spirit to soar. Whether you're seeking heart-stirring solitude or exhilarating exploration, these Polynesian pearls offer an irresistible blend of tranquility and thrill, making them an adventurer's paradise unmatched by any other on Earth.

French Polynesia's Romantic Shores

Nestled in the heart of the South Pacific, French Polynesia is a paradise defined by its enchanting shorelines. Imagine a scene where the horizon melts into turquoise waves and palm trees sway rhythmically in a gentle, caressing breeze. This archipelago, known for its remarkable reef-ringed islands and vibrant marine life, is a dreamscape for those looking to escape the hustle of daily life for a romantic getaway.

Each island in French Polynesia tells its own captivating story. Bora Bora, often heralded as the "Pearl of the Pacific," is a vivid illustration of natural beauty. It's known for the iconic Mt. Otemanu which presides majestically over its crystal-clear lagoon. The dreamy overwater bungalows, unique to these islands, offer a perfect blend of seclusion and luxury, allowing couples to immerse themselves in uninterrupted views of the sea and sky. Here, romance is more than an escapade; it's an experience of time standing still.

The allure of Tahiti, the largest island, is transformative. Though the modern world has left its mark in the city life of Papeete, the outer reaches of the island remain untamed. Black sand beaches skirt secluded coves, and vibrant waterfalls emerge from dense, lush valleys. It's easy to feel the heartbeat of the island's rich heritage in the warmth of local smiles, in the rhythm of the traditional drum beats, and in the exquisite flavors of Tahitian cuisine—particularly the ever-refreshing poisson cru.

As idyllic as it sounds, French Polynesia offers more than just tranquil sips of sunshine and saltwater. Moorea, a short ferry ride from Tahiti, is an adventurer's haven. Its rugged interior teems with hiking trails that promise breathtaking panoramic views, where you can catch sight of dolphins frolicking in the distant surf. For those daring enough to dive beneath the waves, the waters here teem with life. Coral gardens and shipwrecks host myriad species, from vibrant shoals of fish to the graceful gliding of manta rays.

Yet, French Polynesia's true romance lies in its profound simplicity. The islands invite you to slow down, to rediscover the art of doing nothing except watching sunlight dance on waves. As night falls, the sky transforms into a tapestry of constellations, offering a spectacular stargazing experience, free from the world's intrusive lights. It's a time to reconnect—with loved ones, with nature, and with yourself.

The small island of Taha'a, often overshadowed by its more famous neighbors, is a gem for those who seek authenticity. Known as the "Vanilla Island," its scent permeates the air, a gentle reminder of the island's primary export. Coconut groves and pearl farms dot the landscape, inviting visitors to learn and participate. Its shores are less trodden, offering privacy for those sunset walks where the vibrant hues of the sky reflect the telltale glimmer of the water.

Then, there's the barely explored island of Huahine, a place that has preserved its breathtaking beauty and cultural vibrancy away from the glitz. Known as "the Garden of Eden," it captivates with verdant hillsides and aquamarine lagoons. Sacred sites, intricately carved pillars recount ancient mythologies, stand testament to a past that intertwines seamlessly with the present. Visitors often find themselves forming connections with locals as deep as the ocean surrounding them.

On each idyllic shore, the sound of ukuleles and the fragrance of tropical flowers form an enchanting ambiance. It is an invitation to dance—a sway to the eternal symphony of waves and wind, a celebration of life and love on shores where time seems to pause just for you. The charming aura of French Polynesia stirs not only romance but also a profound sense of being part of something timeless and grand.

French Polynesia is more than a destination; it is a rendezvous of dreams. Whether it's the curiosity of newlyweds dreaming of their honeymoon haven or seasoned travelers seeking refuge from the ordinary, the islands promise bliss. It's the kind of place that lingers in the heart, whispers in the mind, and echoes in every fond retelling of the adventures upon return. Irresistibly romantic, impossibly beautiful, French Polynesia waits for dreamers and voyagers alike to find the rhythm of romance amidst its shores.

Remote Retreats in the South Pacific

In a world that's always on the move, where hustle and bustle are constants, the Southern Pacific offers something uniquely different—a serene escape, an untouched paradise. Nestled in the blue embrace of the Pacific Ocean, the remote retreats of this region are not just destinations; they are transformative experiences. They hold a promise, a whisper of tranquility that beckons travelers away from the ordinary and into the extraordinary.

The South Pacific is a mosaic of islands, each with its own character and charm. From the rugged beauty of Vanuatu to the serene atolls of Tuvalu, each island offers an experience that's both distinct and deeply immersive. Imagine lounging under swaying palms, where time moves languidly and serenity wraps around you like a warm embrace. There's an allure in the remoteness—it's isolation that feels more like liberation.

These islands are more than dots on a map; they're vibrant ecosystems teeming with life. Flourishing coral reefs cradle the coastline, a kaleidoscope of color and life. They invite you to snorkel through a world that few get to witness. Beneath the turquoise waves, parrotfish and manta rays glide effortlessly, painting the ocean with vivid strokes. It's a world where the boundaries between land and sea blur, where nature's artistry is on full display.

The islands themselves hold secrets and stories passed down through generations. Local villages offer a glimpse into cultures rich in tradition yet harmoniously attuned to their surroundings. Here, the pace of life is gentle, dictated by the rhythms of the earth and sea. In Fiji, the heartwarming greeting "Bula" is more than just a word—it's a gateway to a culture deeply rooted in community and hospitality.

Nighttime in these retreats is a spectacle of its own. As the sun dips below the horizon, the sky transforms into a canvas of stars—

diamonds scattered against an inky backdrop. There's a comfort in the vast solitude, a reminder that in the grandness of the universe, these islands hold a special place, a sanctuary not just for those who visit but for those who call it home.

Adventure lovers find their own paradise here. The rugged terrains of places like Samoa offer trails that meander through lush rainforests, leading to breathtaking waterfalls that cascade into hidden pools. The thrill of discovery is matched only by the thrill of the landscape itself. Surfers, too, find solace in the perfect breaks of these islands, where waves unfurl with both power and grace.

However, the allure of the South Pacific is equally found in its quieter pursuits. Solitude is a luxury often sought yet rarely found in today's world. Here, you can find it with ease. It's in the sound of the waves lapping against the shore, in the whisper of the breeze through coconut fronds. Here, morning commences with the first light caressing the horizon, and evening is a curtain of quietude draping the day in stillness.

For the romantic at heart, few places capture the soul like these retreats. Honeymooners and couples find themselves wrapped in an otherworldly cocoon of privacy and intimacy. There's a magic in walking down deserted beaches hand in hand, where each step is a promise of endless tomorrows. Even the sunsets seem to linger a little longer, as if they too are reluctant for the day to end.

What's remarkable about the South Pacific's retreats is not just their beauty but the way they remain untouched by time. Many islands have embraced sustainable tourism, ensuring that the natural beauty and cultural heritage remain unspoiled for future generations. Eco-friendly resorts and conservation efforts blend seamlessly with the native landscape, striking a balance between modern comfort and environmental stewardship.

Remote does not mean inaccessible. Many of these islands offer travel experiences that are both luxurious and authentic. Boutique bungalows perched over azure lagoons provide a front-row seat to nature's grandeur. Here, luxury is redefined—not by excess, but by the richness of the experience and the serenity it affords.

These retreats epitomize the spirit of exploration. They celebrate the age-old desire to seek the unknown, to find hidden havens nestled far from modern life's complexity. It's a journey not just to a geographical location, but to an inner sense of peace. Explorers like you are the custodians of these serene paradises, carrying away with you not just memories, but a deeper connection to the natural world and to yourself.

In the end, the South Pacific's remote retreats aren't just about where you go—they're about who you become in the process. They're like a gentle lullaby, a reminder of the simpler joys of life, the beauty of our planet, and the importance of preserving it. Whether you seek solitude, adventure, or a reconnection with nature, the South Pacific is ready to welcome you, with open arms and open skies.

Chapter 11:
The Science of Serenity

In the mesmerizing dance of ocean waves and the soothing caress of warm sand underfoot, there lies an undeniable science to serenity that avid travelers often seek yet barely understand. The rhythm of the tides, a natural balm, whispers calming secrets that transcend the chaos of everyday life. Studies reveal that the salty sea air is rich in negative ions, known to enhance mood and vitality, while the gentle roar of the surf provides a natural soundtrack for meditation and introspection. Time seems to slow as you immerse yourself in these tranquil settings, allowing the mind to unwind and wander freely. Beyond personal rejuvenation, a visit to these coastal paradises also bears responsibility. Awareness of our environmental footprint ensures that these shores remain pristine sanctuaries for future wanderers. By treading lightly, the adventurer not only gains peace but gives back to the land that bestows such tranquility. Let every exploration be an exchange where the warmth of the sun on your skin is met with a promise to preserve the beauty that surrounded you, one peaceful tide at a time.

How Beaches Heal the Mind

Despite the hustle and bustle of everyday life, there's a part of the human spirit that craves serenity and solitude. Often, when we seek that peacefulness, we find ourselves drawn to the ocean's edge. Beaches, with their sweeping vistas and rhythmic waves, somehow have the ability to transform our mental state. The science behind this phenomenon, known as "blue mind science," explores how simply being near water can calm our minds and rejuvenate our spirits.

In recent years, researchers have delved deeply into the effects of oceanic environments on mental health. Studies suggest that the mere presence of water can reduce stress hormones and encourage relaxation. The soothing power of the ocean is not just anecdotal; it's embedded in our physiology. Our bodies are made up of more than 60% water, and perhaps it's the magnetic pull towards the ocean that signals a return to a more balanced state.

Imagine walking along a quiet stretch of sand, feeling the grains sift between your toes, while the sun dapples along your path. Each breath synchronizes with the waves gently crashing on the shore. This rhythmic pantomime of the sea aligns with our own natural rhythms, harmonizing our breaths, heartbeats, and even our thoughts. These experiences highlight what scientists call "restorative environments"— settings that offer significant mental refreshment.

Visiting a beach can provide a sanctuary where the present moment feels palpable, grounding us in a reality that's guided by sensory inputs rather than cerebral clutter. The sound of waves has consistently been shown to lower stress levels, as its frequencies are known to stimulate brain activity similar to that of the meditative state. This phenomenon, often called the "sound therapy of the sea," helps clear the mind of distractions and can lead to profound emotional clarity.

Yet beyond the auditory relaxation, beaches offer a visual feast that promotes mental wellness. The wide horizon and open sky invoke a sense of freedom and expansion that localizes our stresses; what once felt monumental in a closed environment suddenly pales in comparison to the infinite stretch of ocean before us. In this way, viewing vast bodies of water can reset our perspective, shifting our thresholds for anxiety and worry to more manageable levels.

Likewise, the hues and colors of the ocean play their part in cognitive restoration. The color blue, prevalent in oceanic views, is associated with peace and tranquility. We naturally associate these feelings with the ocean's endless landscape, leading to a comforting experience that can balance our emotions. Such visual stimuli encourage the release of dopamine, a neurotransmitter linked to happiness and contentment.

For beach lovers and wanderers alike, this magnetic pull toward the coastline isn't just about a quest for beauty or leisure—it's a pursuit of healing. Jorge Luis Borges once said, "When I read a good book, I long to embark on a journey." Aren't our heart's deepest inspirations found not in cities but on these endless shores where land kisses the sea? Here, where nature's storytelling unfolds, we can uncover untold layers of emotional and mental health.

In connection with the physicality of sands, shells, and pebbles is a form of mindful engagement, where tactile interactions prompt a focus on the present. Building sandcastles, collecting seashells, or simply enjoying the sensation of burying feet in warm, sunlit sand inspires a playful joy, reminiscent of childhood innocence. These simple acts ground us, reminding us of the pleasures present in the world that's right under our feet.

The beaches extend this healing aspect into the spiritual realm as well. There's a communal yet solitary bond that many experience by the sea, one that's wrapped in reflection and contemplation. Whether you're sitting in awe under a sunset's glow, or gazing at the stars' reflections in tranquil waters, the beach provides a backdrop for introspection and emotional soliloquies. Ocean whispers encourage us to leave behind emotional burdens, stitching together a soulful tapestry that reflects personal growth.

Then consider that most underrated of companions—the sea breeze. Ocean air has a unique composition, rich in negative ions that encourage the production of serotonin, a key chemical in the brain for emotion regulation. Taking in a lungful of this air leaves many feeling invigorated yet tranquil, replenished much like the ancient mariners who trusted the winds not just for journeying across seas, but for soul-refreshment too. Are we not all mere wanderers, seeking the ocean's balm to steady our restless hearts?

For adventurers drawn to its shores, each beach visit etches more than just footprints in the sands. These are steps along the path of understanding one's inner peace, of quieting the rat race and tuning into an auditory world of lapping waves and bird calls. These natural symphonies serve as the backdrop to life's grander orchestral score, reminding us of the simpler melodies woven through our complex lives.

Indeed, as research continues to evolve, more advocates of mental health are recommending retreats to waterside environments as part of holistic wellness programs. This tangible link between ocean landscapes and mental clarity suggests that the science of serenity is not just a theory but an avenue worth treading. The gentle mantra of the ocean's waves seems to whisper that healing is within reach, only a beachside retreat away.

In understanding how beaches heal the mind, we find more than a destination; we find a transformative journey. These coastal spaces act as warden landscapes, safeguarding our mental well-being and reminding us of the equilibrium in nature's embrace. As readers unfurl their maps and plan escapes, let the lure of that soothing horizon guide them to places where peace and restoration are not just hopes, but experienced realities. In the dance between sea and shore, travelers might just find the serenity they seek.

The Environmental Impact of Visiting Bays

Standing on the cusp of an untouched bay, one might feel a strong pull towards serenity—a desire to immerse oneself in the symphony of gentle waves and whispering breezes. Yet, with every footprint left in the sand, travelers also tread on the delicate balance between nature and human curiosity.

Bays embody a paradox of invitation and vulnerability. They're cradles of biodiversity, teeming with life both above and below the water. The sheltered waters provide safe harbors for marine life, offering breeding grounds for species ranging from tiny seahorses to majestic sea turtles. However, the very allure that draws us into these natural spectacles also presents a great threat.

Human visitation, while often driven by reverence and appreciation, can unintentionally unleash profound disruptions. Increased foot traffic leads to erosion of delicate shoreline plants that hold the sand in place. These plants are often seen as little more than decoration, yet they serve a critical function in maintaining the structural integrity of the coastline. Without them, the shoreline becomes more susceptible to the erosive forces of the sea.

In addition to physical disturbances, bays frequently face pollution challenges brought about by tourism. Even the most conscientious visitor can inadvertently introduce harmful substances into these ecosystems. Whether it's sunscreen washing off in the surf or a forgotten plastic bottle left behind, pollutants accumulate and wreak havoc on marine life. Fish, mammals, and birds can suffer devastating consequences from ingesting plastics or being entangled in debris.

Beyond the visible impacts, the presence of tourists can alter the social structures and behaviors of local wildlife. Marine creatures accustomed to occasional solitude might change their migratory patterns or breeding habits in response to the unrelenting presence of humans. Birds that nest in nearby cliffs or vegetation might abandon their young if they perceive a threat too near to their habitat.

Moreover, while the immediate environment bears the brunt of tourism pressures, surrounding communities often face changes that ripple far beyond the coastline. The influx of visitors can strain local resources, leading to increased waste production and water usage. Residents feel this pressure not just economically, but culturally as the traditional rhythms of life adjust to accommodate the new demands.

Yet, there's a growing movement towards harnessing tourism's power to positively impact these environments. Eco-conscious travelers increasingly seek out responsible travel practices, exchanging short-term thrills for long-term benefits. By choosing eco-friendly accommodations and tour operators who prioritize sustainability, tourists can help safeguard these fragile coastal ecosystems.

Local initiatives, powered by grassroots efforts and international partnerships, are making strides towards protecting these paradises. Programs focused on educating both visitors and locals about sustainable practices are on the rise. From simple beach clean-up efforts to more complex conservation initiatives, every action counts. When visitors take part in such programs, they leave with unforgettable experiences and a deeper sense of stewardship towards these natural havens.

Furthermore, policy changes are being advocated at governmental levels to regulate and monitor tourism impact. Legislations restricting certain types of watercraft, enforcing strict waste disposal regulations, and implementing visitor limits during peak seasons are few of the measures being explored to balance accessibility with preservation.

As travelers, we hold in our hands not just a guidebook or a map, but a responsibility. The bays beckon us with promises of tranquility and adventure, yet they also entrust us with their continued existence.

It's a delicate dance of respect and restraint, where conscious choices ripple outward with potential to forge a future that's sustainable for bays and all who cherish them.

In this light, visiting bays becomes more than a leisure activity—it transforms into an act of partnership with nature. By traveling with intention, we embrace a stewardship role, ensuring that generations to come will also stand on these shores and hear the reassuring whispers of a serene and vibrant bay.

Chapter 12:
Cultural Tapestry of Coastal Regions

As we wander through the sumptuous coastlines of our planet, we find that each coastal region offers a unique cultural tapestry woven through the rhythms of the sea. Picture walking along a sun-dappled shore where the air is filled with the sound of laughter and the aroma of local cuisines sizzling from nearby stalls. Coastal communities, from the bustling Greek Isles to the serene shores of the Indian Ocean, hold traditions that have stood the test of time, deeply rooted in the ebb and flow of the tides. These traditions manifest in rituals, art, music, and culinary delights that beckon travelers to partake in their stories. Imagine sinking your teeth into freshly caught seafood, expertly crafted with spices that tell tales of faraway lands and historical voyages. In these regions, every wave that crashes ashore carries with it whispers of the past, inviting adventurers to immerse themselves fully and embrace the shared humanity and vibrancy that only coastal cultures can provide.

Traditions by the Sea

In coastal regions around the world, there's a deep connection between the sea and the traditions that shape the lives of those who live there. These traditions, passed down through generations, are rich tapestries woven from the threads of history, culture, and the ever-present influence of the oceans and seas. As you travel to these coastal paradises, you'll find that understanding and participating in local traditions can enrich your journey and offer a sense of belonging, even in distant lands.

Let's start with the rhythmic chants and hypnotic dances of Polynesia, where the oceans not only provide sustenance but also inspire cultural expression. In the islands of Hawaii, the hula dance is more than just a performance; it's a storytelling art that celebrates the gods, legends, and everyday life. The sway of the dancers, the chant of the mele, and the strum of the ukulele have a mesmerizing effect that transports you to another era. Experience the magic for yourself during traditional luaus, where vibrant costumes and fragrant leis bring the festivities to life.

Across the globe in the Mediterranean, the sea dictates the rhythms of life. In Greece, the vibrant celebrations of Easter include processions where the air is filled with the smell of incense and the sound of tolling bells. The tradition of breaking red-dyed eggs symbolizes renewal and is accompanied by the joyful cry of "Christós Anésti!" (Christ has risen!). These rituals are reminders of the enduring connection between the Greek people, their land, and the sea that cradles their ancient civilization.

India's western coastline tells a different tale. Here, in the bustling beaches of Goa, Christianity and Hinduism blend seamlessly during the festival of Shigmo. Diverse communities come together for colorful parades featuring traditional dances called Ghode Modni and Fugdi. The streets vibrate with music as drums beat a frenzied rhythm. This celebration marks the arrival of spring and reflects the multicultural tapestry nurtured by the coast's history as a trade hub.

In South America, coastal traditions are equally captivating. Peru's Pachamama ritual is a sacred ceremony that pays homage to Mother Earth and the sea. Coastal communities gather on beaches to make offerings of coca leaves, chicha (a fermented drink), and fruits to the ocean, honoring the relationship between humans and nature. The vibrant celebration of Inti Raymi, the Incan Festival of the Sun, includes rituals and parades full of color and music, creating a lively atmosphere that envelops both locals and travelers.

In Africa, the coastal regions hold an enchanting assortment of traditions, many of which are centered around the bounty of the sea. Along the Senegalese coast, the annual pirogue races bring communities together in a spirited competition of brightly painted fishing boats (pirogues), rowed by teams of local men. This event harks back to the region's maritime heritage, honoring the skills and courage of fishermen who brave the Atlantic Ocean.

Meanwhile, in Japan, the ancient art of Ama diving showcases an extraordinary tradition practiced mostly by women, known as Ama-san. These "sea women" have been free-diving for abalone and pearls for over 2,000 years. Astonishingly, they dive without any modern scuba gear, relying on their incredible lung capacity and a deep understanding of the ocean. Visitors can learn about their techniques and stories, providing a glimpse into a way of life that is both challenging and beautiful.

The sea is also central to ritualistic gatherings of food preparation, seen in the vibrant, open-air seafood stalls along the shores of Portugal. Here, family and friends converge to enjoy grilled sardines and enjoy good company. It's a simple pleasure, savored at sunset as the Atlantic waves kiss the shore. Such moments capture the essence of maritime tradition—sharing bounty and stories, all against the backdrop of the sea's steady rhythm.

In Northern Europe, coastal communities celebrate the summer solstice with bonfires on the beaches. Known as Midsummer or Jāṇi in Latvia, this event marks the longest day of the year. People gather to sing folk songs, weave flower crowns, and revel in the warm embrace of the midnight sun. These bonfires, believed to scare away evil spirits, create a magical, golden glow that illuminates the shores and spirits alike.

Traditions by the sea are as varied as the landscapes they inhabit. Yet, whether it's the rhythmic beat of a Polynesian drum or the flicker of a European bonfire, each tradition offers insights into a region's history and identity. They are stories of resilience, joy, and the human capacity to adapt in harmony with the ebb and flow of the tides. As you stand at the edge of a new coast, let curiosity guide you to these cultural encounters, where every wave seems to whisper untold stories of the past.

As you traverse these beautiful coastal regions, remember that traditions are living expressions of culture, continuously evolving while retaining their roots in the sacred and the sea. Embrace these traditions, and you may find they offer not just entertainment but a key to understanding the soul of a place. In this sea-bound dance of preservation and celebration, travelers are welcomed as participants in the ever-unfolding narrative of human connection to the oceans that sustain us all.

Culinary Journeys: Tasting the Seaside

The rhythmic ebb and flow of the ocean have long influenced the culinary traditions of coastal regions. As waves crash onto the shores, they leave behind more than just seashells and driftwood. They bring with them a wealth of flavors, aromas, and textures that have been incorporated into seaside cuisines. This chapter takes you on a journey through the vibrant and diverse culinary landscapes of coastal regions, where each dish tells a story of its relationship with the sea.

Coastal dining has a unique allure, marrying fresh ingredients with timeless culinary traditions. Imagine a market bursting with life, where fishermen haul in their day's catch and traders, their hands leathery from the salt air, haggle with chefs and homemakers alike. Stalls brim with an array of vibrant produce, each one holding the promise of a delicious meal. Here, the food itself becomes an embodiment of the ocean's spirit.

There's something inherently romantic about eating fresh seafood by the sea. The salty tang in the air seems to season every bite, making each mouthful a sensory celebration. From Thailand's savory Pad Thai featuring freshly caught prawns to Italy's delicate calamari fritti, the ocean's bounty is honored on plates across the globe. While every coastal region offers its unique flair, they share a common reverence for the sea's gifts.

In the Mediterranean, the emphasis is on simplicity and flavor. The cuisine often features olive oil, garlic, and citrus, with seafood as the star of the plate. Picture a bustling Greek taverna with platters of grilled octopus served with lemon wedges and a sprinkle of herbs. This is a region where meals are cherished and drawn-out affairs, celebrated with family and friends under the glow of the setting sun.

Venture to the shores of Japan, and you'll discover a contrasting palate that embraces precision and artistry. Sushi, an iconic dish deeply rooted in Japanese coastal culture, is more than a meal; it's an experience. Precision in knife work and an emphasis on freshness elevate the simplest of ingredients. Whether you're enjoying a delicate piece of sashimi or a comforting bowl of seafood ramen by the water, the ties to the ocean are unmistakable.

Jambalaya and gumbo swirl with the flavors of the Gulf Coast, melding Creole and Cajun traditions into a savory symphony. Here, the sea's catch mingles with ingredients from the land, creating a vibrant fusion. Shrimp, crab, and oysters are combined with spices, rice, and the famous Cajun trinity of onions, celery, and bell peppers. Each spoonful tells a story of cultural melting pots and a deep connection to the local waters.

In the Caribbean, the vibrant spices and tropical fruits infuse seafood dishes with a warmth and zest that mirrors the islands themselves. Imagine savoring a perfectly grilled fillet of mahi-mahi, marinated in a blend of lime juice, garlic, and fiery scotch bonnet peppers. Here, every meal is a testament to the region's bounty, with flavors as diverse as the cultures that call these islands home.

Coastal eating isn't simply about indulging in flavors; it's a cultural immersion. Food festivals gather communities and travelers alike to partake in long-standing traditions. The Kerala Backwaters food festival in India, for example, offers a chance to explore the intricate dance of spices and seafood that defines Keralan cuisine. Attend a seaside clam bake in New England, and you're participating in a ritual passed down through generations, featuring lobsters, clams, and corn, all steamed together over hot stones under layers of seaweed.

The transformative power of a coastal meal lies in its ability to forge connections: connections to place, to community, and to history. It's about savoring the views as much as the food, with sunsets painting the horizon in shades of pink and gold. It's about gathering around a table with loved ones, engaging in stories and laughter as the sea hums in the background. These meals become more than sustenance; they are the moments that linger long after the journey ends.

Tasting the seaside is to taste nature's bounty, each dish crafted in harmony with its surroundings. Coastal cuisines offer simplicity and complexity, depth and brightness, weaving a rich tapestry of flavors. They invite us into a conversation with the sea, drawing us into a narrative that has been written across sands and stones over centuries. Embarking on this culinary journey is to embrace a part of the cultural tapestry that defines coastal regions, turning every meal by the sea into a map of memories and stories.

So, as you travel to these stunning coastal paradises, let the flavors guide your adventures. Let them whisper the secrets of the sea breezes, the fishermen's early-morning hauls, and the sun-drenched markets offering the day's freshest catch. Let each bite remind you of the deep, enduring connection that we humans share with the ocean and the enduring culinary traditions that have been born from its depths. This is the true spirit of the sea, captured not just in sights and sounds, but in tastes and experiences that nourish both body and soul.

Chapter 13:
Adventures at Sea

With salt tingling our skin and the horizon stretching like a painted canvas, our voyages at sea unveil a tapestry of adventure and romance that words struggle to capture. The call of the azure waters invites us to dive into their crystalline embrace, revealing underwater wonderlands teeming with vibrant life. Each wave carries us to hidden bays where time slows, offering serene sanctuaries for contemplation or spirited sailing. Whether you're navigating the gentle swells of a far-flung archipelago or anchoring in the shadow of rugged cliffs, there's a profound connection forged between you and the vast ocean. It's here, beneath a tapestry of stars or the glowing sun, where dreams are set adrift, and the heart swells with the elation only true explorers understand. Every nautical mile traveled becomes a memory, a story waiting to be shared, inspiring not just wanderlust, but a deeper appreciation for the earth's watery wonders.

Diving into Crystal Waters

Imagine the anticipation as your snorkeling fins grace the edge of a boat, the sea stretching before you like a vast, sapphire canvas. The air is thick with that unique, salty perfume, promising adventures yet untold. Sliding into the cool embrace of the ocean, it's as if you're stepping into an entirely different realm, one where time flows at its own leisurely pace and the everyday worries are merely distant echoes.

Beneath the surface lies a world teeming with life and color, a vibrant metropolis where every hue of blue luxuriates with sun-kissed vibrance. Schools of fish dart in synchrony, kaleidoscopic arrays of scales flickering with the sunlight like precious jewels. The sensation of floating weightlessly alongside these creatures conjures a profound sense of peace. Here, below the waves, nature narrates its oldest, most serene story.

In locations where the waters are supremely clear, the visibility stretches far enough to reveal the shadows of creatures gliding effortlessly through their liquid domain. One moment you're entranced by the sight of a regal sea turtle meandering across a bed of seagrass; the next, you're awed by the sudden encounter with a playful pod of dolphins, their sleek bodies dancing in an arrow-like formation. It's an unspoken invitation to become part of their theater, even if only for a fleeting moment.

For those with an adventurous spirit, diving in these crystal waters unlocks portals to mesmerizing scenes. A descent into the depths presents a near-ballet of marine sensation—a gentle whoosh as air escapes, a fizz of bubbles spiraling upward narrating tales of past dives. The pressure builds slightly but remains exhilarating, heightening your senses and drawing you further into this maritime enchantment. Coral forests rise majestically, coral branches offering shelter for countless sea dwellers, painted by the hand of time.

Explorers find themselves clambering through aquatic nooks and crannies, shifting through light and shadow as they navigate underwater labyrinths. Each crevice and hole tells a tale of resilience and adaptation, of life bowing gracefully to nature's diurnal rhythms. It's hard not to feel humbled in the presence of such intricate ecosystems, where every small creature plays a vital role in maintaining delicate balance.

For those less inclined to venture beneath the surface, the experience of crystal waters still captivates from above. Consider the allure of kayaking over translucent lagoons, where the world beneath unfolds in startling clarity. Rowing steadily against gentle tides, you might catch sight of a manta ray fluttering like an underwater bird. The occasional jolt of a leaping fish reminds you of life's unpredictable charm.

It's not just the abundant marine life that's compelling. The solitude offered by these remote locations creates space for introspection, where the gentle lapping of waves becomes a meditation chant. Surrounded by sea and sky, your perspective grows, encompassing not just the natural beauty of the scene but also an appreciation of your place within it all. The crystal waters ask nothing of you but surrender—to be present, to exist in a state of wonder.

Such locales possess a pulling sense of mystery too. Among veteran divers and marine enthusiasts, whispers circulate of secret spots—a hidden cove here, an undiscovered shipwreck there—safe harbors of the ocean's deepest secrets. These places are prized not for their notoriety but rather for their untamed charm, promising uncharted adventures for those brave enough to seek them.

The enchantment of diving into crystal waters lies not solely in what one witnesses but also in the sensory tapestry that envelopes you. The shift of water temperature as currents embrace you, the surprising textures of coral and stone against a gloved hand, and the laser-sharp focus demanded by underwater navigation all foster an awareness that is rare and rejuvenating.

As you re-emerge from your aquatic odyssey, there's a natural transition from the cocoon of underwater calm to the vibrant energy of day. The sun warms your skin, salty sea drops catching the light as you climb back onto your vessel. The experience lingers, cemented as a cherished memory that will call you back, again and again, to the water's embrace.

In these moments, one understands that diving into crystal waters is not merely a pastime—it's a celebration of life's exuberant diversity and a personal journey into the heart of the Earth's own pulse. Each dive tells a silent story, inviting you to listen, to learn, and most cherished of all, to dive deeper into the boundless wonders of the sea.

Sailing Through Scenic Bays

The gentle rocking of a boat as it slices through the pristine waters of a bay is an experience that touches all the senses. Sailing through scenic bays is an adventure that dips into romantic exploration and the raw thrill of nature's beauty. Imagine gliding past cliffs draped in wild flora, waves lightly kissing the bow, and a horizon infinity of blue. Whether you're steering a sailboat or merely a passenger, the heart races at the promise of hidden coves and untouched shorelines. There's something irresistibly appealing about the unpredictability and mystery that sailing brings—a journey dictated by wind and water, not by rigid itineraries.

Each bay has its own character and story to tell. The luminescent waters of Southeast Asia reveal silken sands beneath, coaxing you into their embrace with promises of discovery. Here, the tranquility of a secluded bay contrasts starkly yet beautifully with the adventurous spirit carried in the salty air. As you navigate these liquid paths, it's easy to lose track of time, mesmerized by the interplay of light and shadows dancing on the water's surface. Each wave and gust of wind carries with it a snippet of histories untold, adventures unplanned.

Dropping anchor in the embrace of a secluded bay offers a unique kind of freedom. The isolation invites a deep connection with nature, a luxury unheard of in the usual tourist rush. These bays, often unreachable by land, guard their secrets carefully, rewarding only the determined sailor with their beauty. Here, it feels like the world pauses. No sounds of the modern world, just the soothing chorus of waves crashing, winds whispering through sails, and perhaps the occasional call of ocean birds. It's in these serene moments that one's mind and soul find an unparalleled peace.

Sailing through these scenic bays also fuels the spirit of adventure and exploration. With each nautical mile, the sea unfolds a chapter of discovery. Will you find a deserted island, untouched by human hands? A hidden waterfall spilling into the sea, draped in a breathtaking verdant backdrop? As an adventurer, the glory of these finds is unparalleled. The sense of claiming a small piece of the earth's wonder, if only for a moment, lingers long after you've left the bay behind.

One can't overlook the interactions with local cultures while sailing. Some bays are the lifeblood of small coastal communities, whose lives are forever intertwined with the rhythmic symphony of the waves. These interactions bring an authentic touch to the journey, where you might exchange seafaring tales with a local fisherman or learn the folklore surrounding a particular bay. Such encounters enrich the sailing experience, painting a fuller picture of life along these beautiful coastlines.

The camaraderie among fellow sailors is another joy of these bay-hopping adventures. Sharing the deck with others who feel the same call of the open sea forges friendships and memories destined to outlast the waves. There's a certain magic in shared sunrises and the collective awe when encountering the surreal beauty of uncharted bays. Stories are swapped over meals, seasoned with salt air and laughter, each tale adding a unique thread to the tapestry of the journey.

Nature's elementals—sea, wind, and sky—are always in command, and it requires both respect and skill to safely navigate them. The dance with the breeze, finding that sweet spot on the sails to catch the perfect wind, is both a challenge and a delight. Each successful maneuver, each safely conquered bay, is a testament to the symbiotic relationship between sailor and sea.

In essence, the act of sailing through scenic bays encapsulates a sense of liberation and discovery. An adventure that can be as tranquil or challenging as one desires, it strips down travel to its core—delving into nature, cherishing moments, and forging connections that transcend the ordinary. Sails billowed with wind and a spirit brimming with wonder; the ocean unfurls stories waiting to be etched into the hearts of those who dare navigate its endless expanse. Within these serene enclaves, dreams are not merely imagined; they're lived.

Chapter 14:
Planning Your Escape

Drenched in the glow of wanderlust and dreams of sun-kissed horizons, planning your escape becomes a thrilling adventure in itself. As you chart your course for the world's most stunning and secluded coastal paradises, every decision takes you closer to tranquility. Finding those hidden gems requires a mix of curiosity, instinct, and knowledge—each step a dance toward solitude and unforgettable beauty. Dive into places where nature's splendor is unspoiled, allowing you to connect with the environment responsibly and respectfully. Let your imagination run wild as you consider the diverse landscapes and cultures that await discovery, every detail whispering the promise of new horizons, fresh adventures, and serene escapes. The sea breezes beckon, carrying on their wings the secrets of places yet unseen and experiences yet unlived. It's time to embark on a journey that will leave footprints on the shores of your soul.

Finding Secluded Spots

In our fast-paced, interconnected world, the allure of finding a secluded coastal spot can be overwhelming. There's something inherently romantic about the idea of discovering a hidden beach, a place where time seems to stop, and the cares of the modern world drift away like the distant waves. The search for these elusive paradises is a journey that promises discovery, reflection, and often, a profound sense of peace. The secret to uncovering these spots lies not in maps or guides, but in a willingness to step off the beaten path and embrace the whispers of adventure.

Start by thinking about what solitude looks like to you. It might be an untouched cove where the only footprints in the sand are your own, or a quiet bay where you can anchor your boat and listen to the gentle lapping of water against the hull. Finding such places requires a blend of intuition and research, a commitment to exploring beyond the obvious. You won't find them in glossy brochures or standard online searches; their very charm lies in their mystery.

To begin your quest, consider local knowledge as your greatest asset. Talk to fishermen, ferry operators, or local shopkeepers; these individuals often hold the keys to undisclosed retreats. Their stories and tips can lead you to places where the landscape is as unspoiled as it was when first set foot upon. When you connect with locals, you gain entry not only to hidden places but also to a richer, more authentic experience of the culture and natural beauty surrounding you.

A willingness to wander off the hurried trail offers an opportunity to find seclusion. Look for paths less traveled, side roads that meander, or boat tours advertised only by a handwritten sign on the dock. Such uncharted territory might lead you to a secluded inlet where you can watch sunsets without sharing the moment with crowds. These are the places that remain ingrained in your memory long after the tan fades and the shells collected have broken.

Yet, the practice of patience is essential. The quest for seclusion might involve detours and dead ends, friendly guides pointing the wrong way, and moments of self-doubt. But isn't the essence of adventure the journey itself? Each wrong turn is merely a reminder of the road less taken and offers stories and lessons that add layers to the experience. Embrace the humor in mishaps, for they'll become cherished anecdotes over time, tales to share with fellow travelers around a shared campfire or dinner table.

As you continue to explore, take time to reflect on the simple joys along the way. Picture yourself sitting on an isolated stretch of beach—it's morning, the air crisp with the promise of a perfect day. The waves pulse rhythmically, and the scent of salty brine mingles with fresh sea breeze. Such moments heighten your senses, tuning them into the quiet symphony of nature's grandeur that surrounds you. In such a setting, you begin to understand the profound power of solitude.

However, as you discover these secluded spots, remember the importance of preserving their sanctity. Carry away only memories—and perhaps a few photos that capture the spirit rather than the specifics—and be mindful not to leave a human footprint behind. Encourage others to follow this same practice, ensuring that these places remain a refuge not only for you but for future seekers of solitude.

If you're traveling by sea, the allure of anchoring off an unnamed island can be irresistible. Imagine snorkeling amid vibrant coral reefs, largely unseen by human eyes, or feasting on a picnic you've packed upon its rocky shores. The song of the ocean and the cry of distant seabirds accompany your thoughts like an ancient lullaby, providing a backdrop for introspection and dreams.

In your search, technology can serve as both a friend and a foe. While GPS and apps might aid in navigation, be wary of their overuse. Allow yourself the sense of discovery that comes from navigating by the sun and the stars, feeling the wind's direction on your skin, and following your instinct. This natural sense of direction often leads to more rewarding discoveries than any screen could suggest.

Consider turning to islands or coastal regions less talked about, places whose names are a mystery even to other travelers you've met along the way. These may be regions where the tourism brochures have only brushed the surface, leaving the true heart of the place undisturbed. Often, a short distance from a busy hub lies a marginal land, unexplored, and waiting in serene splendor.

In this journey to find secluded spots, stay true to what you seek: peace, isolation, beauty untouched by the frantic pace of life elsewhere. Each secluded place found becomes a cherished chapter in your travel memoir, a story to be told and retold, a whisper of the world waiting just beyond the main road.

Tips for Responsible Travel

As you plan your escape to the world's secluded coastal paradises, it's vital to embrace the concept of responsible travel. Not only does this ensure the preservation of these stunning locations for future explorers, but it also deepens your own experience, connecting you to the places and cultures you visit. Responsible travel is more than just a buzzword—it's a commitment to honor and protect the natural wonders that inspire your wanderlust.

Start by understanding the local customs and traditions. Engaging with the culture of a coastal community means more than just enjoying its beaches; it involves respecting its way of life. Spend time learning a few basic phrases in the local language. A simple "hello" or "thank you" in the native tongue can open doors and hearts, fostering an authentic exchange of ideas and smiles. Such gestures not only enrich your journey but also inspire a mutual respect between visitors and locals.

Moreover, when exploring these paradises, step lightly. Stay on marked paths and trails to avoid damaging fragile ecosystems. The flora and fauna of coastal areas are often delicate, and preserving them requires conscious effort. Avoid trampling on vegetation or disturbing wildlife, no matter how enticing it might seem to forge your own path. These small actions contribute to the broader effort to keep these natural wonders pristine.

When packing for your trip, choose eco-friendly and reusable items. Opt for a stainless steel water bottle instead of buying single-use plastic ones. This not only reduces plastic waste but also allows you to stay hydrated during your adventures without contributing to environmental pollution. Reusable shopping bags, bamboo utensils, and biodegradable toiletries are simple swap-outs that make a significant difference. Such sustainable travel habits reflect a deep respect for the places you're exploring.

One delightful facet of responsible travel is supporting local economies. Instead of choosing chain hotels, consider staying in locally owned accommodations or eco-lodges. These options provide a more immersive experience and often come with stories of their own. Dining at local eateries, purchasing handicrafts from artisans, and employing local guides not only supports the economy but also gives you insight into the community's soul.

It's important to be mindful of your environmental footprint. Make conscious choices about your modes of transportation when moving between destinations. Where possible, use public transport, rent a bike, or even walk to explore the area. These methods not only reduce your carbon footprint but often reward you with unexpected gems along the way. You'll find more opportunities to interact with locals, explore hidden alleys, and enjoy the journey as much as the destination.

Engagement with community-based conservation efforts is another way to practice responsible travel. Many coastal areas have initiatives focused on protecting their unique ecosystems, whether through beach clean-up drives, coral reef restoration projects, or wildlife rescue centers. Participating in such activities provides a rewarding sense of contribution and a unique opportunity to learn about the local environment from knowledgeable individuals dedicated to its protection.

Moreover, travelers often overlook the importance of responsible communication about their adventures. Share your experiences in a way that encourages others to travel responsibly too. Social media can be a powerful tool for change, so consider posting about your efforts to minimize your ecological impact. This might include highlighting sustainable practices or posting pictures that showcase beauty without disturbing nature.

Respect the rules of the beaches and bays you visit. Many sites have specific regulations designed to preserve their ecological balance, such as no-take zones, fishing restrictions, or guidelines on interacting with wildlife. Following these regulations is essential, and acting responsibly encourages others to do the same, creating a ripple effect of conservation-minded travelers.

Finally, reflect on the concept of leaving no trace. As much as travel is about discovery, it is also about leaving behind nothing but footprints. Collect any waste you generate and dispose of it properly, ensuring you don't unintentionally spoil the beauty others will come to see. Encouraging fellow travelers to adopt this mindset helps ensure these coastal paradises remain unspoiled for generations to come.

In the spirit of adventure, romance, and pure escapism, responsible travel invites us to be not just visitors, but stewards of the world's most breathtaking places. By embracing these tips, you're taking crucial steps toward ensuring that when you depart, the places you've loved will be just as pristine and magical for the next adventurer seeking the solace of a tranquil shore or the thrill of an azure wave. Remember, it's these responsible actions, both large and small, that weave the lasting tapestry of our shared natural heritage.

Chapter 15:
Coastal Flora and Fauna

In the tapestry of coastal paradises, the story of flora and fauna is a mesmerizing interplay of life and landscape. Every stretch of sand and every hidden bay teems with a vibrant array of species uniquely adapted to the coastal environment. The rustle of mangroves and the whispered secrets of coral reefs form the backbone of these thriving ecosystems. As you wander the shores, keep an eye out for the fascinating oceanic wildlife—playful dolphins, graceful sea turtles, and myriad seabirds that dance in the briny breeze. This biodiverse sanctuary offers a blend of adventure and tranquility, whispering romantic tales of resilience and symbiosis among the surf and saline air. Nature here is not just a backdrop; it's the heart of these sacred shores, calling to those who seek to connect with the raw, untamed beauty that's as diverse as it is enchanting.

Oceanic Wildlife Wonders

Imagine standing on a secluded beach, where the horizon blends into a limitless sky and the sound of waves crashing becomes a soothing symphony. Beneath the surface lies a world teeming with life, vibrant and enchanting—an ecosystem that writes stories older than time. The oceanic wildlife that calls these coastal realms home is as rich and diverse as the colors of a tropical sunset. Let's dive into this spellbinding realm where every ripple and shadow reveals a tale of survival, adaptation, and wonder.

One of the most iconic residents of these waters is the playful dolphin, forever a symbol of freedom and grace. Their striking intelligence and social nature make them favorites among travelers and locals alike. Watching them arc through the water in synchronized harmony is a breathtaking display of nature's choreography. Dolphins often seem to embody the spirit of the sea itself—joyful, mysterious, and ever-moving.

In the quiet shallows of a hidden bay, you might catch a glimpse of a sea turtle gliding slowly, a creature lost in timeless elegance. These ancient mariners chart courses through fierce oceans and find solitude on sandy shores. Their nesting rituals link land and sea, an age-old cycle that invites us to ponder our own place within nature's intricate web. Witnessing the hatchlings' race to the water under the moonlight is a memory etched into the heart, a reminder of resilience against the odds.

Near coral reefs, the oceanic wildlife shifts to a dazzling spectacle of color and movement. Here, schools of fish, resplendent in hues unimaginable, dance among the coral gardens. The symbiotic relationship between fish and coral is a testament to the delicate balance of life beneath the waves. Parrotfish nibble algae with beak-like mouths, their vibrant scales flashing in sunlight—a vivid reminder that life here thrives in diverse forms.

But adventure doesn't end with the coral reefs. Venturing deeper into the waters, the presence of majestic whales transforms the sea into a theater of awe. The sight of a humpback whale breaching is enough to leave even the most seasoned traveler speechless, a compelling narrative of the sheer power and gentleness intertwined in these gentle giants. Their songs, haunting and beautiful, reverberate through the ocean, an eloquent testament to the mysteries yet to be uncovered.

In contrast, along rocky coasts, colonies of seals and sea lions entertain with their antics. Their onshore lazing and underwater acrobatics charm every visitor. These playful pinnipeds are often at ease basking in the sun, while turbulent surf crashes around them. It's a serene chaos that embodies the essence of coastal living, a realization of life's ability to carve a niche even in the harshest environments.

Further offshore, in colder climes, nature challenges explorers with its stark grandeur. The icy waters become a stark canvas where penguins waddle from ice to the sea with an unhurried elegance and seals evade orcas in a primal game of predator and prey. Here, the raw, powerful narrative of the ocean's wilderness plays out—a reminder that life, in its endless variety, knows no bounds.

As tidepools recede with the ebbing tide, another universe is exposed. Here, starfish cling patiently to rocks, while anemones sway like delicate dancers. These small, captivating worlds captivate young and old alike, transforming curiosity into a refuge of discovery. The colors and textures offer an accessible gateway to oceanic wonders without venturing deep into the sea—a natural gallery of marine artistry.

Marine birds add their own dynamics to this sea of life, soaring and diving with unrivaled precision. From the stately albatross, with its monumental wingspan, to the rapid dives of pelicans, their presence is a sight to behold. Coastal cliffs and islands serve as bustling colonies, where breeding rituals play out in magnificent displays and harmonize with the crashing waves below.

Further enriching this mosaic of ocean life are the often-overlooked heroes: the microorganisms—plankton and krill—serving as the foundational sustenance for countless marine creatures. These tiny organisms glow ethereally under specific conditions, offering a visual spectacle of bioluminescence that turns the surf into a shimmering, magical dance of lights. Their impact, though felt far less directly, shapes the health of the entire ecosystem.

While embracing the magic of oceanic wildlife, we must also acknowledge the roles we play in these stories. Travelers attracted by the pull of ocean wonders are uniquely positioned to be stewards of its future. By observing marine wildlife with respect and meeting conservation efforts with enthusiasm, each encounter can become a pledge to protect this fragile paradise.

In coastal paradises around the world, from the calm lagoons of French Polynesia to the rugged coasts of Northern Europe, oceanic wildlife weaves a rich narrative that demands exploration and conservation. Their beauty is timeless, yet the responsibility to ensure such wonders endure falls upon us. As we seek inspiration and solace in these remarkable ecosystems, let's remember they're not just backdrops to adventure, but vital, living worlds in need of our care and admiration. Let us move forward, inspired by the oceanic wildlife wonders, ever committed to preserving the life that gives our oceans their timeless allure.

The Role of Mangroves and Coral Reefs

Mangroves and coral reefs are nature's sentinels, standing guard along our planet's coastlines. These vibrant ecosystems not only adorn our shores with their beauty but also provide vital protection and sustenance to the flourishing flora and fauna they shelter. As you find yourself traversing the world's most stunning coastal edge, understanding the role of these natural wonders enriches your journey and enhances your appreciation for these fragile yet formidable guardians.

Imagine walking barefoot on a secluded beach, the Earth underfoot seemingly firm and resilient. Yet, hidden beneath this enchanting serenity is an intricate web of life, anchored by mangroves and coral reefs. They form a symbiotic relationship with the coastal environment, where each element depends on the other, creating a tapestry of resilience and abundance that beckons explorers who seek both romance and adventure.

In warm coastal regions across the globe, mangroves flourish with determination. They rise gracefully from the shallows, their roots weaving into intricate networks that embrace the coastline. These roots are not just the foundation of the mangrove tree but are homes to myriad species. Crabs scuttle along their submerged branches while fish dart through their protections, seeking shelter from predators. For the beach lover and adventurer alike, venturing into these tangled forests offers a glimpse of a world where life thrives untamed, unencumbered by human interference.

Mangroves are remarkable not only for their biodiversity but also for their ability to shield coastlines from the fury of the sea. Their roots stabilize the shore, reducing erosion and buffering against storm surges, working silently to keep coastal paradises intact for generations to soak in their splendor. Understanding their protective role encourages travelers to become stewards of these delicate ecosystems, acknowledging that every footprint and ripple can have lasting effects.

Further offshore, beneath the glinting surface of the azure sea, coral reefs paint the ocean floor with colors that captivate the soul. These underwater rainforests are the epitome of beauty and complexity, serving as both refuge and nursery for myriad marine species. From the smallest shrimp to the grandest rays, life here is an intricate ballet of survival and harmony that invites exploration and evokes awe.

Imagine diving into the depths, greeted by the sight of clownfish dancing among the stags of coral or the slow, majestic glide of a sea turtle on a timeless pilgrimage. This is a realm where silence sings a song of life, and every discovery sparks a sense of adventure in the hearts of those intrepid enough to explore below the waves. Each visit is a reminder of our planet's wondrous complexity and brings a call to action to preserve these marvels for those who will follow in our swim-finned steps.

Coral reefs are undeniably a crucial buffer against coastal threats. They dissipate wave energy, protecting shorelines from erosion and flooding, making them an unsung hero of our seaside sanctuaries. Beyond their physical sustenance, these reefs also represent a wellspring of inspiration and creativity, often reflected in the music, art, and stories that arise from cultures entwined with the sea.

The interplay between mangroves and coral reefs sets the stage for a thriving aquatic theater where life unfolds with dazzling splendor and strategic design. Tourists, adventurers, and nature lovers drawn to these locales find their experiences deepened by this connection. Behind the scenes, mangroves filter nutrient-rich waters, feeding the coral reefs while serving as the first line of defense against pollutants. This cyclical relationship ensures that both ecosystems continue to flourish, supporting everything from the playful dolphin to the majestic frigatebird.

As you journey through these breathtaking landscapes, take a moment to consider the unseen forces at play. Stand amidst mangrove roots or dive among coral heads, and recognize that you are witnessing one of the planet's most resilient collaborations. It's an adventure through time and nature, where each moment spent immersed in these surroundings enriches our understanding of the interconnectedness of life.

In understanding the role of mangroves and coral reefs, we're gifted with a deeper appreciation for the beauty and complexity of our coastal paradises. As stewards of these environments, our travels can transcend mere observation and evolve into a commitment to preserving the world's secluded shores. In respecting and protecting these pristine locales, we ensure that their wonders remain untouched, ready to inspire and enchant the travelers of tomorrow.

Chapter 16:
Under the Stars

As the sun dips below the horizon, a different kind of magic awakens along the world's most secluded coasts. The embrace of the night brings a serene and enchanting allure to these hidden gems, where sandy shores become the stage for nature's grand performance. Lie back and let the rhythmic cadence of the waves lull you into tranquility while the sky unfurls its glittering tapestry above. In these moments, the universe feels within reach, each star a beacon of wonder guiding your thoughts to distant realms. Whether you're warming yourself by a cozy beach fire or simply enjoying the solitude, there's a profound connection to be found under this vast canvas of night. In the hushed whispers of the ocean and the twinkling constellations, you can discover stories as old as time itself, and perhaps, even a story of your own. Here, under the stars, the world seems to pause, offering an invitation to dream beyond the ordinary, to find inspiration in the solitude, and to let the beauty of the cosmos ignite the wanderlust within your heart.

Nighttime Beach Experiences

Imagine the edge of the world where the sea meets the sand, both aglow under the silvery embrace of the moon. This is the magic that awaits you at nighttime beaches, places where nature crafts its most poetic symphonies after the sun has bid adieu. The rhythmic beating of waves against the shore is a timeless lullaby, soothing your soul and inviting your mind to wander through the mysteries of the night.

As dusk transitions to darkness, beaches transform into a stage for nocturnal wonders. On some shores, the phenomenon of bioluminescence steals the show. This captivating light show is created by millions of tiny marine organisms that emit flashes of light, making the ocean glow with an ethereal blue hue with every brush of the waves. It's a living masterpiece, a rare opportunity to walk along a shimmering path of liquid stars, leaving footprints in an otherworldly glow.

Yet not all nighttime beaches are about luminous wonders. In some parts of the world, the simple beauty of a moonlit beach is enough to stir hearts. Walking hand in hand under the starlit sky, your only company the nocturnal creatures that emerge when the world is at rest. The symphony of night—the whisper of the breeze through palm fronds, the distant call of an owl, the rhythmic chant of the ocean—provides the perfect score for an intimate connection with nature.

Forging deeper connections with nature is just one of the myriad experiences nighttime beaches offer. They invite solitary explorers to lose themselves in contemplation, the vastness of the ocean serving as a mirror reflecting your innermost thoughts and dreams. The absence of daylight skims away distractions, allowing the essence of the beach to speak louder—its scent, its sounds, its feel. It's a personal retreat, offering clarity where there once was chaos.

And if adventure calls, nighttime beaches respond in kind. There's the thrill of nocturnal swimming in the warm embrace of tropical waters, or the exhilaration of kayaking over a bioluminescent bay, your vessel leaving a trail of light in its wake. Perhaps the call of a midnight picnic speaks to you, with a lavish spread that echoes the richness of the night—wildberries, aged cheese, and a good bottle of wine to toast the silence that envelops you.

For those drawn to the spiritual, nighttime beaches can offer a different kind of journey. Many have been the backdrop to ancient rituals, where the ancients gathered to invoke blessings from the sea. Standing on these hallowed grounds, you can feel the timeless connection to those who came before. It's a place to meditate, to ponder, and perhaps to leave small offerings—a flower, a seashell, a whispered hope to be carried by the tides.

In community gatherings, the nighttime beach can be a playground of joy and revelry. Bonfires light up the shore, and stories passed down through generations come to life. Laughter mingles with the crackling of wood and the chorus of nighttime creatures, creating a tapestry of sound under the vast sky. Everyone becomes part of this mosaic, dancing shadows against a backdrop of infinite possibilities.

Technology has a way of darkening the skies with constant light and noise, but the nighttime beach remains a space where time slows, and the noise dissipates. It's a realm where digital connections fade in favor of human connections and true serenity. Under the blanket of stars, the worries of the modern world seem far removed, giving way to a pure, untainted experience of nature's grandeur.

There's also an element of mystery to nighttime beaches, an allure that promises secrets shrouded in the moonlight. While the shoreline might look familiar in daylight, the night reveals a different face. Shadows create new shapes and forms, inviting exploration and discovery. It reminds us that beauty exists in the unseen, urging us to embrace the adventure that lurks in the unknown.

As night waltzes towards dawn, the experience of a nighttime beach lingers, tattooed on your memory like a gentle reminder of nature's marvels. The first light of morning may wash away the shadows and return the world to its ordinary palette, but the spell cast by the night remains. It's a gentle nudge towards a quieter soul, an inspiration that lasts long after the waves have erased the night's footprints.

So, whether it's quiet reflection, an exhilarating adventure, or the embrace of shared laughter, nighttime beaches offer something for everyone. They're an invitation to witness the world in its most intimate state, a call to step away from modern distractions and immerse yourself fully in the embrace of nature's nocturnal spectacle. Venture to these shores under the stars, and let yourself be swept away by the magic of the night.

Stargazing from Secluded Bays

The dance of the cosmos is free for all to see, but there is something uniquely enchanting about experiencing it from the intimate setting of a secluded bay. Far removed from the glaring lights of cities, these hidden coastal retreats offer an unspoiled canvas where the universe can unfurl its starry tapestry in all its glory. It's as if nature herself conspires to provide a front-row seat to the celestial show, enhancing the adventure with a sprinkle of romance and introspection.

Imagine settling down on a plush swath of sand, backed by the gentle lullaby of waves. It's in this peaceful isolation that time seems to pause, and the sky reveals itself in its truest form. Stars that remain hidden in urban settings burst into brilliance over secluded bays, their light weaving patterns that tell stories as old as time. The Milky Way stretches across the sky like a grand, celestial river, leading your thoughts to drift and wander.

There's a primordial lure to lying under such a vast expanse, where countless civilizations before us looked skyward and fashioned myths to explain the wonder above. In these bays, far from the hustle and bustle, one feels a gentle reminder of our place in the universe—both humbling and freeing. It's the perfect setting for a moment of personal reflection or sharing dreams whispered under the stars.

These bays are more than just settings; they transform into sanctuaries where the night sky becomes a gateway. Picture it: the silhouette of towering cliffs framing the night, casting long shadows that mingle with the moonlit surf. As you gaze upward, planets come into focus, and constellations reveal themselves like old friends. It's as though the earth itself sighs contentedly around you, enveloping you in its gentle strength.

In the stillness, there's a conversation that requires no words. It's in the soft rustle of leaves, the crash and retreat of the tide, and the harmonious chorus of nocturnal creatures. Overhead, meteors streak across the sky, momentary flares that leave you blinking in awe. You feel the air's crisp coolness, a perfect contrast to the warmth of the sand beneath you. It's an intoxicating blend of the natural elements that nourishes the adventurer and the dreamer alike.

For the romantic at heart, these experiences are more than simple pleasures; they become cherished memories etched into the fabric of your soul. Holding a loved one close, wrapped in a blanket beneath the starlit canopy, there's a shared intimacy that brings hearts together in ways few settings can. Each star seems to glow brighter, enhancing the connectedness one feels under that vast, twinkling sky.

Secluded bays, with their undisturbed shores, offer a unique opportunity for uninterrupted stargazing while sparking an adventurous spirit. There's a thrill in discovering these hidden gems, reaching places where maps don't always lead you. Whether accessed by rugged trails or quiet waterways, the journey to these bays is part of the allure. The adventure lies both in the getting there and the quiet epiphanies found once you've arrived.

Stargazing in these remote locations isn't just for the astronomers or seasoned adventurers; it's an invitation extended to anyone willing to take a pause and look up. Whether you're a seasoned traveler or a curious novice, the open arms of these secluded spots wait to cradle even the most casual stargazer. And while equipment can enhance the experience, the sheer naked-eye view of the constellations often suffices to inspire wonder and awe.

Even as the night whispers its secrets, time stretches out, obbligato to nature's rhythm. Suddenly, the familiar outlines of Perseid or Orion morph into reminders of our shared human history—a bridge connecting generations. Therein lies the magic of these moments, in which the stars watch over the timeless dance of life lapping against the shores.

For those yearning to experience such stargazing magic firsthand, planning helps. Check lunar calendars for new moon phases, when the absence of moonlight unveils an even clearer celestial view. Research conditions of ideal bays and prepare for a variety of climates because whether it's a warm embrace of a tropical breeze or the brisk air of a northern retreat, the sky's grandeur extends its grace over all.

It's not just the stars that capture attention in these quiet enclaves. The reflection of celestial bodies on the tranquil waters of a bay can enhance one's experience, doubling the impact and leaving a lasting imprint on the heart. Here, nature paints not just across the vast sky but in the gentle ripples of the water too, doubling the intensity of a beautiful moment.

As the bay cradles you in its arm, the comfort of the sands and the music of the waves fosters a tranquility that beckons you into a serene slumber, only to be gently awakened by the first whispers of dawn. Here, under the retreating stars and the watchful eye of a rising sun, a transformation completes—a metamorphosis of the nocturnal magic into the day's possibilities.

In the end, perhaps it's this profound blend of mystery and familiarity that makes stargazing from secluded bays a timeless escape. As the sky turns on its axis and offers these windows into eternity, we're reminded that while the universe is vast, it's also deeply personal. It beckons both the solitary wanderer and the company-seeking romantic, inviting everyone to take part in the dialogue between earth and sky.

Chapter 17:
The Evolution of Coastal Landscapes

As waves kiss the shorelines and sculpt the rugged edges of the earth, our coastal landscapes are under a ceaseless transformation, an artistry born from the interplay of natural forces and time. This evolution is not just about erosion or the rambunctious dance of tides; it's a tale steeped in history, where each grain of sand holds stories of its own journey through the elements. The coasts, whether they're brimming with vibrant tourism or remain untouched and secluded, stand as testaments to both nature's resilience and fragility. Exploring these landscapes, we see more than shifting sands and receding lines— we witness islands disappearing, peninsulas being carved anew, and beaches that transform not just in shape but also in spirit. This dance speaks to the adventurous soul, inviting us to marvel at nature's relentless creativity while pondering the ever-changing tapestry we are fortunate to walk upon, for amidst these changes lies an enduring beauty waiting to inspire the wanderer in all of us.

Understanding Coastal Erosion

Coastal landscapes are more than just places to relax with the sun on your face and the sand between your toes. They're dynamic, ever-changing canvases marked by the patient artistry of nature, where the elements come together to craft awe-inspiring scenes over time. Coastal erosion, a natural process central to this transformation, is both artist and destroyer, sculptor and eraser, playing out its eternal drama at the edge of continents and islands alike.

Picture a cliffside battered by waves bearing the relentless force of the ocean; over years, perhaps centuries, it crumbles, evolving into something new. This is coastal erosion—a process driven largely by the wind, water, and human activity. As romantic as it sounds to watch nature run its course, the reality is that erosion can dramatically alter coastlines, impacting both the natural beauty of the area and human activities and homes.

Now imagine walking along a sandy beach, admiring the way the shore gently curves towards the horizon. These tranquil landscapes often owe their existence to the ceaseless work of erosion, wearing away rock formations and depositing sediment along the coast. It's a cycle of loss and renewal. Each high tide carries a little more of the coast into the sea, while each low tide may reveal new sandbars or reshape a familiar bay.

Erosion is most dramatic where the land is made of softer materials like clay or loose sediments. The pounding waves, unrelenting and tireless, wear away the base of a cliff until it's undercut, causing large sections to collapse dramatically into the sea—a destructive act that paradoxically contributes to the creation of new landscapes. These materials are then carried by ocean currents to new locations, perhaps to form a sandbar or an extended beach somewhere further along the coast.

But it's not only nature that has a hand in molding coastlines. Human activities significantly accelerate erosion, turning once leisurely processes into direct threats to coastal communities around the world. We build barriers against the sea, install drainage systems, and construct homes on vulnerable cliffs—all underestimating the power and persistence of erosion. Seawalls and groynes may temporarily prevent the sea's encroachment, but they also disrupt natural sediment flows, causing unexpected consequences down the coast.

The romance of coastal landscapes is steeped in their mystery and unseen battles. They are testaments to the power of geological and oceanographic processes, where the land surrenders piece by piece to the rhythmic dance of the waves. Coastal erosion isn't a mere scientific phenomenon; it's part of the stories these landscapes whisper to those who wander their shores.

As a traveler, understanding coastal erosion enhances not just your appreciation of nature's handiwork but also instills a sense of responsibility. You are a guest in these spaces of wonder and fragility, and with this understanding comes the importance of responsible interaction. It offers insight into why certain areas might be roped off or why paths are redirected—every effort works to preserve what erosion slowly takes away.

In this grand orchestration of natural forces, erosion not only shapes coastlines but also plays a crucial role in supporting a variety of ecosystems. Tide pools, salt marshes, and estuaries owe their existence to the movement of sediment, creating habitats that are rich in biodiversity and integral to the health of marine life. Coastal erosion's artistry reveals layers of ecological significance that sustain life, from the smallest organisms to complex underwater ecosystems.

The flinty resolve of the sea, steadily reclaiming land, can inspire a deep introspection. We might ask ourselves how this forces us to adapt, how it urges us to cherish the temporary forms it leaves behind—cliffs, beaches, and dunes that are there for now, but may not be for future generations.

As we wander these landscapes—whether exploring the jagged cliffs of Northern Europe, lounging on the sun-kissed beaches of French Polynesia, or adventuring in the remote retreats of the South

Pacific—we should remember: coastal erosion is as much a part of their beauty as the sunsets and surf. It's a reminder of the transformative power of nature, a call to appreciate both the fleeting and the enduring. Treasure these places and embrace the adventure of discovering what lies beyond the next tide.

The Changing Tides of Tourism

As the world grows ever more connected, the ebb and flow of tourism create ripples that transform the coastlines we cherish. Travelers, drawn to the allure of sand and sea, shape these idyllic locales in myriad ways. Coastal tourism, once a privilege for the few, has become accessible to the many. With this accessibility comes change, sometimes subtle, often profound, yet always impacting the landscapes we love.

In earlier times, coastal adventures were the reserve of the adventurous, those willing to brave the unknown in search of beauty untamed. Grand voyages brought the first glimpses of distant shores to delighted eyes. Today, a click of a button launches a thousand journeys, each traveler with the potential to rediscover what had once been hidden. This shift in accessibility has undoubtedly spurred a tourism boom, inviting more people to experience the magic of coastal paradises.

Tourism has become a double-edged sword, fueling opportunity while threatening to sever the delicate balance of nature. On one hand, it's a lifeline for local economies, providing income, infrastructure, and international recognition. Local communities find themselves at the intersection of tradition and innovation, adapting to meet the desires of curious visitors.

But there's another side to this story. Coastal areas face unprecedented challenges, from environmental degradation to the cultural shifts that accompany vast numbers of visitors. Communities must grapple with preserving their identity and sustaining their environments, often through trial and error. The changes brought on by tourism can appear like an intricate dance, where each step forward might necessitate a careful step back.

Technology, while enabling this global discovery, also plays a crucial role in managing its impact. Digital platforms offer tools for responsible travel, educating tourists on best practices as they thread lightly through pristine environs. These tools, coupled with a growing consciousness for sustainability, represent hope for maintaining the treasures that draw the world's darers and dreamers.

Coastal destinations also find themselves at the forefront of cultural exchanges. The shores that once inspired solitude now echo with the voices of many, each visitor bringing elements of their own culture to the mix. This fusion creates a rich tapestry unique to each locale, as local customs blend with global influences, crafting destinations where anyone can feel at home.

The pandemic has also given this dynamic a fresh perspective. With travel restrictions came a pause, an unprecedented opportunity to reflect on tourism's path. As borders reopen, travelers and locals alike ponder how to forge a future that honors nature rather than overwhelms it. This global pause has nudged many toward more mindful exploration, appreciating the untouched and lesser-known, valuing quality of experience over quantity of destinations.

Global and local efforts to protect coastal regions have begun to reconcile the needs of tourism with the imperative of conservation. Initiatives that empower communities to steward their resources promise to transform tourism from a potential threat to a force for preservation. Areas like the Great Barrier Reef have championed eco-certification programs that highlight sustainable practices, encouraging businesses and travelers alike to engage responsibly.

Yet, amidst these challenges, coastlines stand resilient, adapting to the tides of change. In this intricate dance, there exists an underlying truth: the beauty of coastal landscapes and the experiences they offer are constant, unyielding to the passing fads of generations. Their timeless allure remains intact, continuing to captivate and entice the human spirit.

The future of coastal tourism depends not just on policies and practices but on the decisions each traveler makes. Embracing authentic experiences, respecting the delicate ecosystems, and cherishing the cultural fabric woven through sandy shores can redefine tourism's impact. The call to action lies not just with those who own or operate these havens but with every visitor who steps onto their sands, leaving footprints and taking memories.

In the end, the evolution of these amazing landscapes speaks to the broader narrative of connection—between humans and the natural world, between communities and travelers, and between the past and a sustainable future. As travelers become more aware of their footprints, both literal and metaphorical, the tides of tourism may yet shift again, this time toward a harmonious and enduring relationship with the world's most spectacular coastal gifts.

Chapter 18:
Inspiring Stories from the Shore

As the sun dips below the horizon, painting the sky in hues of pink and gold, the shore becomes a place where dreams and reality blur, creating stories that inspire wanderlust and adventure. These sandy stretches host tales of locals, like the guardian of a secluded bay in Greece who's kept the beach pristine for generations, believing in its powers to heal and renew. Travelers, too, have their stories—like the solitary backpacker who found unexpected companionship in a remote cove in Thailand, and the couple whose romantic sojourn on a Caribbean island became an eternal memory etched in their hearts. Each story is a testament to the profound connection between humans and the ocean, a reminder of the beauty and mystery that lie just beyond the shore, waiting to transform those who dare to explore.

Guardian of the Beach: Local Legends

The world's coastlines are alive with stories that ripple through generations, much like the waves that kiss the shore. Among these tales, the "Guardians of the Beach" stand out as vibrant, flesh-and-blood legends. These are the local heartbeats of coastal communities—figures who embody the spirit of their beaches, dedicating their lives to protecting and preserving the sand-strewn sanctuaries they've always called home.

Imagine stepping onto a secluded beach, the salty breeze wrapping around you like an embrace, when suddenly a voice echoes down the shore. That voice belongs to someone like Aunty Nani, a Hawaiian elder who knows every grain of sand on her beach. Aunty Nani strolls along her beloved stretch, her feet rhythmically sinking into the wet earth. For decades, she's been the unofficial steward of the cove, sharing whispers of ancient stories with any willing to listen. Her serenading tales remind us that these shores are sacred places, repositories of tradition and wonder.

In the buzzing vibrancy of Rio de Janeiro, another guardian emerges amidst the energetic hum of beachgoers: a jiu-jitsu master simply known as Mestre. He finds solace in his dawn patrols across the sands of Copacabana, his eyes scanning the horizon, watching over both locals and travelers with a protective spirit. To this day, Mestre helps keep the beach clean by organizing early morning groups focused on collecting litter—a mundane but vital task that sustains the natural beauty of these shores.

Across the ocean lies Africa's western coast, where the legendary Mamadou dedicates his days to the preservation of Senegal's wild beaches. His face weathered by the elements, Mamadou embodies resilience and wisdom. Once a fisherman, he realized the detrimental impacts of overfishing and now leads a community initiative to promote sustainable practices. His footprints stretch across miles, a reminder to all who follow that one person can indeed make a difference.

Iceland's northern reaches offer another tale, where the enchanting Sólveig, an accomplished marine biologist, carries the torch as a beach guardian, though her tools are science and education. She's spent her life studying the fragile ecosystems within the frigid embrace of the North Atlantic. When she speaks with tourists drawn to the shimmering black sands of Reynisfjara, her passion transforms simple conversations into inspiring calls to action.

Then there's Tane from New Zealand, a man whose connection to his family's stretch of coastline runs as deep as the roots of the mighty pōhutukawa trees. Tane's forefathers sailed these waters, and he carries on their legacy—teaching younger generations the stories and songs that hold the essence of their Maori heritage. His tales aren't just heirlooms; they're a living history ensuring that tradition thrives amidst modernity.

What all these figures share is an unyielding devotion to the landscapes they hold dear. Their voices, each distinctive and powerful, weave a tapestry of stories surrounding these jewels of nature. They're reminders of how our planet's coasts offer more than mere sunbathing locales; they are theatres of dreams, history, and heroism.

Personal connections with nature often inspire others to take up the mantle of guardianship. Among travelers who've been touched by the sincere energy of beach guardians are those who return home, inspired to protect their local natural spaces. It happens when the romance of the ocean leaves an imprint, nudging these visitors to act, to become protectors of their miles of forgotten coastline or inner city parks.

It's not just the guardians' commitment that's compelling, but the unspoken bonds they form with those who tread onto the sands they call home. Their stories whisper in our ears like the sea's gentle roar, offering encouragement that we, too, might find ways to protect and cherish this planet's paradisiacal edges.

As you explore the world's shores, take a moment to seek out these guardians. Strike up a conversation or join in their efforts, understanding that each beach carries its own legends, its own protectors. Whether it's safeguarding wildlife, sharing cultural knowledge, or simply maintaining a pristine environment, the guardians' work is a reminder of the collaborative effort required to preserve such beauty for generations yet to come.

Travelers' Tales: Journeys to Paradise

As the tide ebbs and flows, so do our desires to wander and explore the vastness of the world's coastlines. Every beach, every shore, holds a tale—a story whispered by the waves, carried by the salt in the air, waiting for adventurers like us to discover. In this chapter, we dive into the stories of intrepid souls who set forth on journeys to find their quintessential paradise. Their paths, though unique, share a common thread; the irresistible pull of the sea and the promise of serene sunsets over golden sands.

One such tale is of Lisa and James, a couple who found each other on the windswept shores of the Algarve in Portugal. Having met while backpacking through Europe, they bonded over a shared love of the ocean. By day, they explored the craggy cliffs and hidden coves, while at night, they camped under the starlit sky, lulled to sleep by the rhythmic lapping of waves. For them, the Algarve was not just a destination but a backdrop to their unfolding love story—a slice of paradise that will forever be etched in their hearts.

Across the world, in the tropical embrace of Thailand's Similan Islands, another tale unfolds. There, a solo traveler named Ahmed, weary from the chaos of city life, sought refuge among the pristine sands and warm azure waters. These islands, a diver's Eden, offered him an escape—a sanctuary where he could swim alongside sea turtles and vibrant coral gardens. Amidst the marine life, Ahmed found a quiet resolve and the clarity that had eluded him back on land. His journey became one of self-discovery, illustrating that sometimes, the greatest adventures are the ones that occur within.

Then there is the story of Mei and Hana, two friends who embarked on a road trip along Australia's Great Ocean Road. Their journey was not only about the destinations marked on a map but also about the spontaneous detours and unexpected encounters along the way. From the mesmerizing rock formations of the Twelve Apostles to the sleepy coastal towns they passed through, every turn was an invitation to explore. Their laughter echoed above the roar of the ocean as they reveled in the freedom and joy of discovery.

Not all journeys to paradise involve sandy shores. For Sven, a devoted surfer, paradise was found in the chilled waters off Iceland's rugged coast. There, beneath the shadow of towering cliffs and beneath a sky that danced with the auroras, he rode waves that challenged his skills and ignited his spirit. Iceland's stark beauty and raw power made each ride an exhilarating reminder of nature's grandeur. Sven's tale is one of embracing the elements and finding beauty in the unexpected.

The stories of those who venture to the world's sublime coastlines are as varied as the shores themselves. They reflect our innate desire to connect—with ourselves, with others, and with the natural world. These travelers teach us that paradise is not merely a place, but an experience born from the journey itself. Whether seeking solace, adventure, or the thrill of discovery, the sea offers an eternal promise: a canvas on which to paint our dreams and write our stories.

As we conclude our exploration of these inspiring tales, let us remember that paradise is a realm we create as much in our hearts as in the destinations we pursue. For in every grain of sand and each crash of wave, whispers the promise of endless exploration and the hope of stories yet to be told.

Chapter 19:
Protecting Our Coastal Paradises

As our journeys have taken us from the sunlit shores of Greece to the wild bays of New Zealand, the importance of preserving these natural wonders has become increasingly clear. The vivid imagery of palm-fringed coastlines and the soothing lull of the tide compels us to pause, reflect, and take action. It's not enough to merely visit these paradises; we must become stewards of their future. Conservation efforts are blossoming, with local communities leading the charge to defend fragile ecosystems against climate change and pollution. Supporting sustainable tourism initiatives isn't just a trend; it's a necessity to ensure the awe-inspiring beauty we've cherished can be savored by generations to come. By choosing eco-conscious travel options and participating in beach clean-ups, we do more than just preserve; we participate in the enduring tale of the world's coasts, a narrative written in the whispers of ocean breezes and the vibrant hues of coral gardens. Let's embrace the role of guardian and savor every untouched grain of sand with the knowledge that our travels leave more than footprints—they contribute to a legacy of protection and love for our seaside havens.

Conservation Efforts and How to Help

Our endless fascination with coastal paradises is as old as humankind itself. The lapping waves, the whispered promises of the sea breeze, and the mystical outline of distant horizons have long fueled our collective wanderlust. While these natural wonders continue to inspire our journeys, they also demand our stewardship. In embracing these breathtaking coastlines, we are called not just to revel in their beauty but to protect their fragile ecosystems. This section is dedicated to exploring conservation efforts and outlining how each of us can contribute to preserving these irreplaceable treasures.

Conservation along coastal paradises spans an array of initiatives, from large-scale governmental projects to grassroots community movements. At the forefront are the countless marine protected areas (MPAs) established worldwide. These zones aim to manage and safeguard marine ecosystems, ensuring that creatures and plant life can thrive unimpeded by human intervention. Successful MPAs can dramatically increase biodiversity, support sustainable fish populations, and even boost local economies through eco-tourism. While some have been more effective than others, their ongoing evolution and optimization provide a critical blueprint for future conservation efforts.

But it's not just MPAs that play a pivotal role. Innovative conservation programs blend scientific research with traditional knowledge, looking to coastal communities for guidance. It's a reciprocal relationship: as locals share their insights and customs, scientists offer technological support and data analytics to enhance conservation strategies. Around our beloved shores, this harmonious partnership unfolds with stories like reef restoration projects wherein communities actively cultivate and transplant coral, hoping to reinstate vibrant underwater gardens.

To facilitate these efforts, technology stands as both a powerful ally and a guiding force. Drones, satellite imaging, and AI now allow researchers to monitor coastal changes and identify critical areas for intervention, while mobile apps enhance citizen science initiatives. These tools empower individuals to become active participants in conservation, enabling beach-goers and adventurers to document wildlife, record pollution levels, and promptly report violations. Imagine snapping a picture of a fluke from your boat and contributing to global whale tracking—each action, however small, impacts the greater conservation tapestry.

The movement isn't complete without acknowledging the wisdom of indigenous peoples, whose traditional practices often include sustainable coastal management techniques passed down through generations. When coupled with modern conservation practices, these age-old methods foster approaches that are equally effective and mindful of cultural heritage. Collaborations with indigenous communities have led to some of the most sustainable conservation models, exemplifying respect for nature as a living legacy shared among all who tread its paths.

As travelers, the transformation from passive observers to proactive participants forms the essence of responsible tourism. Understanding the impact of our footprints—literal and metaphorical—encourages mindful travel. Choosing eco-friendly accommodations, participating in beach clean-ups, or engaging in environmental education experiences during our trips are practical ways to contribute. These choices not only honor the destinations we visit but also kindle a global culture of sustainable travel.

Education remains the axis around which all conservation revolves. Knowledge empowers action. Experiential learning through interactive exhibits, virtual dives, and conservation-oriented tours fuels our curiosity and deepens our connection with the oceanic wonders. When we comprehend the delicate balance sustaining these paradises, the imperative to preserve them becomes personal and immediate. Every adventurer, whether a student on a gap year or a retiree exploring newfound freedom, carries the capacity to spark change.

While initiatives abound, funding remains a perennial challenge. Many communities lack access to essential resources needed to realize their conservation goals. This is where non-profit organizations and individual donors play a crucial role. Supporting causes such as mangrove restoration or bycatch reduction—efforts which protect habitats and minimize unintended marine life captures—not only funds essential projects but also raises awareness. Crowdfunding platforms now make it easier than ever to contribute to grassroots conservation efforts, enabling even small donations to create a ripple effect.

Your voice, too, holds power. Engage in conversations about conservation, advocate for policies that prioritize ecological preservation, and use social media to share stories of change and inspiration. The more we dialogue about these issues, the more we bolster collective understanding and action. After all, our treasured coasts are not distant or abstract spaces; they are integral threads in the intricate weave of global ecosystems, and our stories are tied to theirs.

Looking ahead, climate change presents the most formidable obstacle, threatening to unravel the meticulous conservation work undertaken. Rising seas, warming temperatures, and acidifying oceans alter ecosystems and endanger countless species. Resilience, adaptability, and innovative approaches are essential to countering these impacts. Developing adaptive strategies and bolstering natural coastal defenses—like dunes and wetlands—are crucial pieces of this evolving puzzle.

So, what does this mean for you, the traveler, the dreamer of coastal paradises? It means embodying a spirit of guardianship, transcending the role of a mere visitor. By investing your time, resources, and energy into conservation, you become part of a thriving community committed to ensuring that future generations might wander these same paths, enchanted by their beauty but also inspired by the stories of those who cared enough to preserve them.

The call to action is clear. Embrace the adventure and romance of beaches and bays with a profound commitment to their preservation. For in safeguarding these paradises, we don't just protect the sands beneath our feet or the seas that serenade us; we nurture the very essence of what it means to be a traveler, one who seeks the world not just as it is, but as it could be—glorious in its natural splendor, sustainable in its enjoyment, and enduring in its legacy.

Sustainable Tourism Initiatives

In our quest to explore the world's most stunning coastal paradises, it's essential to tread lightly and prioritize sustainability. Sustainable tourism has emerged as a beacon of hope, ensuring that the allure of these paradises remains undiminished for generations to come. But what does this entail for adventurous souls seeking to leave only footprints, and perhaps a positive legacy, behind?

One central aspect of sustainable tourism is minimizing the environmental footprint of travel. This involves choosing accommodations that prioritize eco-friendly practices. Many coastal resorts now integrate sustainable measures into their operations, such as using renewable energy, reducing water consumption, and managing waste effectively. Travelers can support these initiatives by opting to stay at establishments committed to sustainability. It's a small action with a large impact.

Furthermore, the concept of slow travel is gaining traction. Instead of skimming the surface by hopping from one destination to another, slow travel encourages visitors to immerse themselves more deeply in fewer places. This approach not only enhances the travel experience but also reduces the carbon footprint associated with frequent travel. Imagine lingering longer on Greece's pristine beaches or enjoying extended stays exploring the secluded bays of Costa Rica. It's about quality over quantity and experiencing destinations authentically and responsibly.

Yet, sustainable tourism is not solely about minimizing harm. It's also about actively contributing to the well-being of local communities. This can be accomplished through community-based tourism initiatives, which empower local populations by creating jobs and fostering cultural exchanges. Rather than conventional mass tourism, which can disrupt local ways of life, community-based tourism invites travelers to engage personally and meaningfully with residents, adding depth to their journeys.

Consider this: purchasing handcrafted souvenirs directly from artisans not only supports their craft but also sustains cultural heritage. Participating in local tours or workshops enriches understanding and provides a platform for cultural exchange. Travelers become part of the story, not just spectators.

Another key component of sustainable tourism involves ensuring that local flora and fauna are respected and preserved. A growing number of organizations and destinations offer eco-tours that educate visitors about the local ecosystem and conservation efforts. For instance, guided tours through coral reefs emphasize the importance of protecting these delicate marine environments. Such experiences cultivate appreciation and inspire travelers to advocate for environmental stewardship long after their trip ends.

In areas rich with biodiversity like the Philippines' islands or Africa's Indian Ocean beaches, conservation-focused tourism helps to raise awareness and often directs funds to critical conservation projects. By engaging in activities led by knowledgeable guides, adventurers gain insights into the interplay between human activity and natural habitats, grounding their travel in a deeper context of preservation.

Moreover, sustainable tourism initiatives often extend to the culinary domain as well. Embracing locally sourced food not only reduces carbon emissions but also supports the local economy. Dining at restaurants that utilize sustainable seafood practices or visiting local markets offers a genuine taste of the coastal culture and provides visitors an intimate look at the everyday life of the locals.

That said, travelers should be mindful of the balance between enjoying the beauty of coastal paradises and understanding their fragility. Awareness and education are vital in promoting responsible behavior. Many destinations have introduced visitor education programs, aiming to inform travelers about the environmental and cultural importance of the areas they are exploring. This knowledge empowers travelers to become ambassadors for sustainable travel, continuously mindful of their impact.

An inspiring example can be seen in the effort to combat plastic pollution. Many beaches now participate in regular clean-up drives that travelers can join. This hands-on involvement not only collects litter but fosters a sense of responsibility. As adventurers pitch in with local efforts, they contribute to preserving the pristine beauty of the shorelines they cherish.

Ultimately, supporting sustainable tourism initiatives comes down to informed, conscious choices—choices that acknowledge the connection between tourism, culture, and environmental conservation. It requires an understanding that, as visitors, we carry the responsibility to protect the very destinations we're drawn to.

The movement toward sustainable tourism is more than just a trend; it's a necessity. As coastal paradises face pressures from climate change and human activity, the role of the traveler transforms from that of a consumer to a steward. Embracing sustainable tourism allows us to continue exploring with a sense of respect and wonder, ensuring these paradises remain sanctuaries of beauty, peace, and adventure for those who will follow.

Chapter 20:
The Spirit of the Ocean

In the heart of every traveler lies an undeniable pull toward the ocean, a call that resonates with whispers from the depths of time itself. These waters, vast and teeming with life, are where myths come to life amidst the crashing waves—a mermaid's song, perhaps, or the legendary kraken stirring from its slumber. The ocean's spirit melds with something within us, a sense of freedom and wonder that fuels our desire to explore, to understand our small yet significant place in this great aquatic ballet. There's an ancient energy that swirls around those who walk the shorelines, transcending the physical separation between land and sea. It invites reflection and connection, a spiritual kinship with the rhythms that have long shaped humanity's journey. Whether it's the solemnity of witnessing the sun dip beneath a horizon painted with hues that defy description or the gentle lull of waves offering solace, the ocean's spirit echoes our own, reminding us of life's perpetual ebb and flow. As we delve into its mysteries, we find ourselves not just traveling across its surface but journeying deeper into our own souls, where tales of the deep intertwine with dreams uncharted.

Myths and Legends from the Deep

In every corner of the globe, the ocean has whispered tales into the ears of those daring enough to listen. These myths and legends, born from the swirling depths, capture humanity's imagination and tether our dreams to the world's vast waters. They're not just stories; they are windows into the soul of the sea itself, blending fact, fantasy, and the timeless dance between them. One can't help but feel both small and profound when faced with such narratives—figments of the unknown, breeding awe in our hearts.

Among the most famous tales of the deep are the mysterious mermaids, enchanting yet dangerous. Legends of these alluring creatures find their origins in the ancient annals of maritime lore. Mariners spoke of enchanting sirens with voices so captivating they led sailors astray, steering their ships toward the jagged cliffs along the stormy coasts of Greece and beyond. Whether myth or misunderstood encounters with marine life, the thought of these beings populates the dreams of anyone who gazes too long into the sea's endless horizon.

Travel further, to the Pacific Islands, where legends murmur of the great Polynesian navigators and their deep spiritual connection to the ocean. It's said that the voyagers could feel the currents beneath their canoes and read the stars like a map stretched across the night. These mariners were guided not by compasses, but by knowledge passed down through generations—a testament to how intimately connected they were with the sea's whispers and the myths that sang through the salty air.

The legend of Atlantis, an advanced utopian civilization swallowed by the sea, continues to capture imaginations worldwide. Plato's tales set the stage for countless explorations and theories about where this lost city might lie. Could it rest beneath the Mediterranean waves, or perhaps in the vast expanse of the Atlantic? The course of time may blur the lines of fact, but the mystery of its existence lingers, urging explorers and dreamers to speculate and search.

In the icy waters of Scandinavia, tales abound of the Kraken, a massive sea creature capable of pulling entire ships under with its long, tentacle-like arms. Sailors from the Nordic regions spoke of these behemoths as living storms, lurking beneath the tranquil surface of the ocean. The Kraken, terrifying yet captivating, stirs the adventurous spirit within, a reminder of the sea's unparalleled power and the mysteries that dwell beyond our understanding.

Then there's the heartfelt tale of Sedna, the Inuit goddess whose tragic story reflects the ocean's dual nature as both life's source and its fierce protector. Angered by her father, Sedna plunged into the Arctic seas, her fingers creating seals, whales, and the myriad creatures that populate the cold waters today. Her story reminds us of the reverence indigenous cultures have for the sea and the delicate balance it holds in sustaining life.

The tale of Davy Jones, a fearsome spirit said to rule the sunken realms, has seeped into popular culture, gripping audiences with its dark allure. Said to harbor the souls of those lost at sea, his locker remains a chilling reminder of maritime dangers. Yet, there's something undeniably romantic about this myth too—it's a tragic nod to the brave souls who've ventured into waters unknown, their stories never to be told but forever captured by the waves.

Across the African coastlines, one finds tales of Mami Wata, the water spirit depicted as both nurturing and tempestuous. This paradoxical figure embodies the dichotomy of the ocean: its capacity to nourish life and wreak havoc with equal measure. Mami Wata stories are woven into the cultural fabric, influencing rituals and beliefs, underscoring the ocean's profound significance in these communities.

Japanese folklore tells of the Umibozu, enigmatic sea spirits known for their temperamental appearances during storms. These giant, shadowy figures rise suddenly from the seas to challenge sailors with riddles, demanding tribute. It's believed that by the clever providence or respectful offerings, sailors could appease these spirits, continuing their voyages unharmed. The Umibozu remind us of the delicate interplay between man and nature, stressing respect and humility in the face of the ocean's might.

As we journey through these legends, a pattern emerges: the ocean, with its vastness and mystery, becomes a canvas for human imagination. Each myth, whether born from fear, curiosity, or reverence, is a narrative thread that weaves us into the tapestry of the world's waters. These stories not only entertain but serve as ancient compasses, guiding us back to times when nature was inseparable from our day-to-day lives.

Perhaps there's a modern-day parallel to draw here, one that speaks to explorers of today's world. In pursuit of the secluded coastal paradises scattered across the globe, we too dance with the spirit of the ocean. These myths spark a sense of adventure within us, coaxing us to explore, respect, and cherish the moments forged at the boundary of land and sea. They whisper of lessons learned and adventures untold, nudging us to honor the call of the ocean's mystery.

Ultimately, these myths and legends remind us of the timeless bond between humanity and the sea. As the waves lap gently at our feet, they carry with them echoes of ancient tales and new possibilities—a siren call to forever explore the world's stunning shores and the profound stories that dwell beneath the ocean's glittering surface.

Spiritual Connection to the Sea

The sea, a vast expanse of mystery and beauty, beckons to us with whispers of serenity and timelessness. It holds a powerful allure that transcends its physical presence, touching the realms of the spiritual and the eternal. For centuries, many cultures have regarded the ocean as a sacred entity—a wondrous force that connects the temporal world with the divine. As travelers and adventurers stand upon the shore, gazing out at the horizon where sky meets sea, they tap into an ancient wellspring of wisdom and peace that invites reflection and introspection.

Venturing to the world's most secluded coastal paradises offers more than just visual satisfaction; it provides an immersive experience of spiritual renewal. The rhythmic lull of the waves, steadily crashing against the shore, acts as nature's meditation, guiding weary souls towards tranquility. Here, in the gentle embrace of the tide, one can find solace and clarity, as the sea unfailingly demands presence and mindfulness. Each breath drawn to match the rhythm of the ocean speaks of liberation and a simplified existence, away from the cacophony of daily life.

Cultures around the world impart deep spiritual significance to the sea, considering it both a source of life and a realm of mystery. In Hawaiian traditions, Kanaloa, the god of the ocean, plays a role not only as a divine figure but also as a symbol of open communication and profound knowledge. Similarly, for the Māori of New Zealand, Tangaroa, god of the sea, signifies unity and continuity, representing both the feared and the cherished aspects of life. These stories envelop the ocean in a mysticism that adds layers to our experiences when we seek to connect with these waters.

As adventurers carve paths across varied coastlines, the ocean stands as a backdrop to moments of personal revelation. The salty breeze carries not only the scent of the sea but the potential for transformation. There are tales of life-altering encounters with the ocean's vastness—from solitary night vigils on a moonlit beach to contemplative moments of sunrise revelations. Each experience brings its own unique spiritual insight, echoing the ancient sailors whose horizons expanded to match the limitless sea before them.

There's a remarkable fellowship shared among those who seek the ocean's cradling arms as a place of spiritual nourishment. This deep connection often extends to communal gatherings, traditional celebrations, and rituals by the sea. Many cultures hold ceremonies that honor the sea's bounty and express gratitude for its role in sustaining life. In these sacred moments, people are reminded of their smallness in the face of the colossal ocean, yet simultaneously, there's an unyielding sense of interconnectedness—a cosmic dance where each wave, each grain of sand, plays its part.

The contemplative nature of the sea invites questions that delve into the core of our existence. What does it mean to truly live? What are the essential elements that enrich our lives? Staring across the endless waves, one may ponder the virtues of patience and adaptability inherent in the tides, the lessons of humility taught by the ocean's immensity, and the acceptance of our transient nature as reflected in the sandcastles by the shore, fleeting yet beautiful in their brief existence.

Adventure by the sea encourages us to listen—not just to the sounds of nature but to the deeper voice that speaks within. This inner dialogue, inspired and softened by the sea's presence, can guide the soul toward its true north. Those who have felt lost often find themselves at the edge of the ocean, where answers aren't served on a golden platter but rather whispered in the breeze, revealed gently in the froth of waves that retreat, leaving behind insights scribbled upon the sand.

The ocean's spiritual embrace is not limited to those who journey physically by its side. Anyone touched by its stories, its images, and its legends can feel this connection. Art, music, and literature often channel the sea's mystical allure, perpetuating its significance far beyond geographical constraints. The ocean's spirit flows through verses and melodies, reminding us of its omnipresence and its ability to inspire those who dare to listen to its enigmatic harmonies.

At the heart of this spiritual connection lies the realization that the ocean reflects the infinite possibilities of the self. It encourages exploration, both outwardly across untamed waters and inwardly towards undiscovered depths of the soul. As travelers wander farther, there is an unspoken understanding that the sea holds a piece of them—a heart that beats in rhythm with the waves, attuned to the universe. With every journey that begins or ends by the seaside, a new chapter of self-discovery and harmony is inscribed in the chronicles of one's spirit.

For those who seek the unexplored and the serene, venturing to the ocean's edge offers not just an escape but a return. A return to simplicity, to truth, to the elements of life that are genuine and authentic. In the salty matrices and under the watchful gaze of the endless tide, they may find not just a destination but a home—one that transcends physical boundaries and speaks to the soul with an ageless, comforting promise of belonging.

Chapter 21:
Beach Dreams and Ocean Whispers

As you stand at the edge of the world where the sand meets the salt and the horizon seems to sing a lullaby, the ocean whispers secrets of distant lands and forgotten dreams. Here, where the waves compose a symphony that echoes the heartbeats of countless wanderers before you, inspiration flows as freely as the tide. The world's artists have long found muses in these coastal retreats, crafting poetry and melodies that capture the rhythm of the sea's embrace. Each gust of wind carries notes of serenity and adventure, melding together in a harmonious blend of beauty and mystery. There's an undeniable romance in the way the waves kiss the shore, a narrative told in the language of the tides. Close your eyes, and let the soft roar of the ocean guide your imagination, painting visions of unexplored paths and endless horizons. This is where dreams are born from whispers, where every crash of surf breathes life into the art of living. The beach is not just a place; it's a feeling, a canvas of infinity calling you to embrace the infinite possibilities of tomorrow.

Poetry and Art Inspired by the Sea

As the sun dips below the horizon, the sea becomes a canvas of endless possibilities. An artist's palette unfolds in the sky—a dance of vibrant oranges, pinks, and deep purples reflecting upon the water's surface. This spectacle has inspired countless artists and poets, from ancient times to today's modern creatives, to delve into the mysteries and beauty of our planet's vast oceans. The interplay between light and shadow, the mesmerizing motion of waves, and the whispers of the ocean breeze weave stories waiting to be told.

For poets, the sea holds a unique allure. It's a symbol of freedom and turmoil, reflecting our innermost feelings. Consider the way the ocean speaks, its language a series of waves crashing rhythmically on the shore. It stirs the soul, inciting emotions that demand expression. Whether it's the calm of a glassy sea or the roar during a tempest, the ocean evokes powerful imagery and presents a metaphor for life's grand adventures.

Many find their muse in the solitary embrace of the beach. An empty stretch of sand, untouched, invites contemplative solitude. Sitting on a weathered piece of driftwood, the universe feels both vast and intimate. It's here that inspiration flows. Lines of poetry emerge, capturing the ephemeral nature of waves lapping at the edge of the land. Words coalesce into poems that speak of romance—the sea is a passionate partner, eternally dancing with the shore.

In the realm of visual arts, the sea offers an ever-changing subject. Painters have long been captivated by the challenge of capturing the transient beauty of oceans. From J.M.W. Turner to Winslow Homer, artists have attempted to paint the sea's restless energy. Each brushstroke is a tribute to the complexity of colors that the sea, clouds, and sunshine create together.

Imagine a painter standing on a rocky outcrop, canvas in hand, gazing out over a rugged coastline. The sea churns below in a spectrum of blues, greens, and whites. With each wave, a story is told, and it's the artist's task to immortalize these fleeting moments. An evening sky, heavy with hues of sunset, finds its way onto a canvas, trapping light in brushstrokes that breathe.

The tactile experience of creating art by the sea also nurtures a connection between the creator and the element. Sculptors, for example, fashion forms from materials eroded by saltwater and time. The tactile crunch of wet sand being molded into a sandcastle, or the careful chisel of a seashell onto driftwood, connects the artist to nature's raw materials. These creations stand as ephemeral art under the sun, soon to be reclaimed by the sea.

In literature, the sea serves as both setting and muse, drawing readers into universes where reality and fantasy intermingle. Stories rise and fall like waves, with each narrative arc reflective of the endless luminescence of the sea's horizon. There's Hemingway's "The Old Man and the Sea," where the struggle against the vast, unexplored ocean becomes both plot and philosophy. It's a poignant reminder of man's enduring spirit against nature's might.

Consider the song of the ocean, rhythmically crashing against cliffs as if to punctuate the verses of existence itself. The symphony of the sea contributes to the artful dance of poetry. It helps bring to life stanzas that speak to love and loss, joy and despair. A well-crafted poem about the sea often becomes a verbal painting, each word brimming with color and sound.

Poetry and art inspired by the sea connect us with the deeply engrained human experience of exploration and discovery. In their creations, artists and poets encapsulate the ever-changing nature of the ocean, turning the mutable into something eternal. As travelers and adventurers, we find solace in these works, feeling the same call to the sea that they felt—a beckoning to explore, to understand, and to celebrate.

Art by the sea encourages collaboration and conversation among cultures that have been touched by the ocean's magic. Different interpretations and artistic expressions from around the world unveil the universal appeal of the sea. Whether it's Japanese ukiyo-e depicting serene coastal landscapes, or the vibrant, swirling colors of Polynesian art illustrating their deep bond with the ocean, each region brings its own voice to the shared narrative.

The sea's influence on art and poetry is not only historical but continues to evolve. Modern artists, armed with digital mediums, reinterpret the sea's timeless allure through photography, digital illustrations, and multimedia installations. These new mediums allow for a broader audience to experience the ocean's majesty in innovative ways, capturing subtleties that might escape the naked eye, such as the iridescent scales of fish gliding below the surface.

Even sculptors engage in ephemeral performances with the sea as their stage. Their works, sculpted from seaweed, sand, and shells, are displayed on the tide's terms, eroding and shifting with each passing wave. These transient sculptures serve as poignant reminders of our connection to, and dependence on, the sea—nature's greatest masterpiece.

The ocean continues to inspire a myriad of artistic expressions, a timeless mirror reflecting humanity's innermost emotions. Whether you're standing on the shore with pen in hand or contemplating the colors on your canvas, the sea provides a wellspring of creativity. For the traveler, the artist, the dreamer, the sea beckons with whispers and dreams, urging us to dive into its depths to uncover the stories it holds.

Music of the Waves

There's something inherently magical about the rhythmic sound of ocean waves crashing against the shore. This phenomenon, often referred to as the symphony of the sea, holds a mysterious allure that has captivated human hearts for centuries. Each wave, a musician in its own right, contributes to a timeless melody that dances with the wind and kisses the sand. It's a concert with no composer, yet it resonates with a harmony that speaks directly to the soul.

The music of the waves isn't just a backdrop to a day at the beach—it's an invocation, a call to immerse oneself in the moment. It's the universe's way of saying, "Pause. Listen. Breathe." For the adventurer and the seeker, this unending song invites exploration not just of the physical world, but of an inner landscape as well. Each wave is a tempo change, a rhythm unique unto itself, unwritten yet precisely constructed by nature's hands.

The waves create their own kind of language. To those who wait, who listen closely, they tell stories. Each crest carries whispers from afar, tales of distant lands, and ancient secrets hidden in the depths. They sing of voyages completed and journeys yet to come. They echo with the adventures of seafaring old and the dreams of those who long to return to their serene embrace.

For many, the waves serve as muses. Artists have forever been inspired by their rise and fall. Musicians and composers find that the ocean's natural melodies influence their compositions, striving to capture a piece of that grand symphony in their own work. Often, the goal is not to replicate the sea's music but to accompany it, allowing one's art to flow in tandem with the waves' seamless, eternal concert. In this dance, creativity finds its highest form—fluid, elusive, and deeply moving.

The sounds of the ocean can influence our state of mind. There's a scientific basis to this—it's been shown that the steady rhythm of the waves can induce a meditative state, calming the mind and reducing stress levels. This isn't just an emotional response; it's physiological. The brainwaves begin to synchronize with the rhythm of the swell, a natural lullaby that lulls us into relaxation. For the wanderer drawn to the water's edge, this music becomes a tool for healing, a way to reconnect with both the natural world and one's own interior landscape.

For the romantics among us, the music of the waves is a serenade for the senses. Imagine walking along a moonlit beach, the waves' gentle song interwoven with the soft rustling of the wind through palm leaves. It's a setting ripe for dreams to unfold and stories to unravel, one where thoughts flow as freely as the tide. Whether strolling hand in hand under a starry sky or alone, pondering life's wonders, the ocean's melody accompanies every step, turning moments into memories.

On some beaches, the particularly unique wave formations create sounds unlike any other. The thunderous roar of a powerful surf during a storm, or the serene, almost imperceptible lap of water on a quiet lagoon at dawn, each provide a distinct sonic experience. The way the sound changes as the weather shifts illustrates the ocean's dynamic nature, a reminder that life, too, is about adaptation and flow.

The interaction of water and soul is an ancient bond. Coastal tribes and civilizations have revered the ocean for its musical qualities for millennia. They saw in it a reflection of their own stories, the highs and lows of survival, celebration, and change. The waves were considered both a gift and a guide—a presence that deserved reverence and understanding.

There's a reason why people are often drawn back to the beach, year after year. It's not just the sun and sand that call to them, but the promise of that ever-present symphony. For some, the ocean's music sparks a sense of adventure. It's an endless pursuit of new places where the waves sing slightly differently, yet each beach shares in the universal hum of nature's chord.

To those who have ever stood on a cliff overlooking a vast ocean, feeling small but profoundly connected to something greater, the music of the waves is the earth's reminder of continuity. It plays as much today as it did in times long past, uniting travelers and explorers across generations. As you wander the coasts of the world, whether well-trodden or hidden, let the ocean's music be your guide. Listen with an open heart, and perhaps you'll find the inspiration you've been seeking.

So pack your bags and set sail not only for the vistas awaiting you but for the soundscapes that promise to soothe and invigorate. Whether you're chasing adventure or solace, remember that the waves are ever-ready to share their music. In their song lies the beauty of the unseen, the rhythm of life, and the promise of endless horizons.

Chapter 22:
Beyond the Beach: Inland Exploration

While the shimmering coastline often takes center stage in our travel dreams, venturing inland reveals a tapestry of experiences that can inspire the soul in unexpected ways. Just a stone's throw from sandy shores, lush forests and rolling hills invite the adventurous spirit to discover hidden waterfalls and expansive vistas. Meandering trails lead to charming villages where local traditions offer a rich tapestry of culture, as vibrant markets and centuries-old temples paint a vivid picture of life beyond the ocean's edge. Whether climbing rugged cliffs to find breathtaking panoramas or savoring the earthy aroma of fragrant vineyards, the inland escapade promises an intoxicating blend of nature's grandeur and cultural richness. Here, away from the familiar whisper of the waves, the land's heart beats with a rhythm just as serene, yet infinitely compelling. The allure of coastal exploration is deepened, reminding us that true adventure knows no borders.

Discovering Hinterland Wonders

As much as the lure of azure waves and endless stretches of white sand can capture our imaginations, there's a world waiting beyond the beckoning shorelines that often remains unexplored. Venturing inland from these coastal paradises, you'll find the hinterlands teeming with their own kind of magic. Landscapes undulating with hills and valleys, cloaked in vibrant greens or rugged stone, offer a serene counterpoint to the vibrant blues of the ocean. These inland wonders are part and parcel of the coastal experience, unveiling layers of beauty and intrigue that call to the adventurous spirit.

The hinterlands offer a richer palette for those willing to move beyond the sandy borders. Often overshadowed by their beachy counterparts, these areas pulse with life and legends. The lush greenery of tropical rainforests, with their towering canopies and symphonic wildlife, invite you to adventure into the heart of nature. Hiking trails whisper with the secrets of ancient landscapes and the promise of breathtaking vistas. Each step reveals a vibrant tableau—a story written in the language of flora and fauna unique to the region.

In regions such as Costa Rica, the juxtaposition of coastal and inland wonders is especially striking. Here, the transition from beach to rainforest is seamless. Just a short drive away from the ocean's roar, you'll find yourself enveloped by a symphony of birdcalls and the rustling of leaves overhead. Nature reserves and national parks preserve the integrity of this incredible biodiversity, where the rhythm of nature flows unhindered.

Traveling inland can also mean a journey through time. Scattered across these landscapes are cultural treasures that reveal the rich tapestry of human history intertwined with the land. From the mystical Mayan sites in Central America to the ancient castles hidden in Europe's highlands, the hinterlands tell stories of past civilizations that once thrived far from the sea's edge. These sites, often nestled amidst breathtaking scenery, offer a different kind of exploration—one of the mind and spirit.

For those enamored with flora, the inland regions serve as a living library. Exotic plants and trees, some of which may seem otherworldly, stand as testament to the planet's diversity. They're not just a feast for the eyes; these plants play crucial ecological roles, supporting wildlife and ensuring the health of the planet. Botanical gardens and natural reserves provide insight into the delicate balance that sustains life.

These places invite contemplation and inspire a deeper appreciation for the intricate connections woven through our world.

Adventurers seeking more physical pursuits will find ample opportunities in the hinterlands. From rock climbing rugged cliff faces to kayaking down wild rivers, these landscapes are playgrounds for the daring. The thrill of cresting a mountain peak rewards climbers with panoramic views that stretch to the coast, reminding us of the sea's continual presence, even when mountains stand between us.

The hinterlands are also birthplaces of culinary innovation. Inland towns and villages, often thriving with local markets, pride themselves on farm-fresh produce and traditional methods. Here, you can taste the land's bounty in hearty dishes that reflect both history and the unique ecosystems from which they are drawn. Culinary trails offer a taste tour, allowing visitors to experience local flavors crafted by artisans skilled in their trades.

Yet, exploring inland isn't just about the stunning scenery and tantalizing cuisine. It's about the connections forged along the way. The people who call these places home often share stories and offer insights into their relationship with the land, deepening your understanding of the bond between humans and their environment. Every conversation is a chance to learn, to grow, and to see the world from a different perspective.

Travelers often find themselves lingering longer than expected, captivated by a beauty that transcends the coastal allure. It has a way of inviting reflection, of grounding you in the present moment. As your journey through the hinterlands unfolds, you'll come to appreciate the seamless connection between sea and land—a duality that enhances the experience of each.

In a world where paths less traveled hold the richest rewards, discovering inland wonders becomes a journey of the soul. The memories formed amid towering forests, undulating hills, and age-old cultures become treasured stories—whispered back to the sea as a testament to the adventures taken and the wonders found. So, while the sands of the coast may draw you in with promises of leisure and sun-kissed relaxation, remember the hinterland's call. It isn't just what lies inland that makes it remarkable; it's how these journeys shift our focus, invite introspection, and allow us to carry both land and sea in our hearts.

Cultural Sites Near Coastal Areas

Exploring coastal regions is often synonymous with basking under the sun or diving into azure waters. Yet, beyond the sandy stretches and whispering waves, a vibrant tapestry of cultural heritage awaits. These coastal areas house history-rich sites embodying the spirit and stories of civilizations that have thrived by the ocean's edge for centuries. A journey into these realms offers more than a traditional beach escape; it presents an opportunity to delve into the soul of these regions, where land meets sea in a confluence of culture and natural beauty.

In the Mediterranean, coastal towns such as Dubrovnik and Split in Croatia are not only known for their pristine beaches but also their historical significance. Dubrovnik, with its formidable city walls, tells tales of a maritime city-state that stood resilient against sieges and storms. Walking through its cobblestone streets, you are invited to imagine life during the height of the Republic of Ragusa—a place where the air would have been filled with the scent of salt and the songs of sailors.

Journey further east to Turkey's Aegean coast, and you'll find Ephesus, home to the grand Temple of Artemis, one of the Seven Wonders of the Ancient World. Though only ruins remain, wandering through this site conjures images of its former glory. The juxtaposition of temple stones against the blue skies creates an evocative landscape that echoes with the whispers of ancient traders and thinkers who once congregated here.

On the other side of the world, the coastal areas of South America offer their own remarkable pasts. Peru's northern coast is home to Chan Chan, the largest pre-Columbian city in the Americas. This complex of adobe brick structures was the heart of the Chimú Empire, and walking through its remnants offers a glimpse into an intricate society that flourished long before the arrival of Europeans. Nearby, the coastal cities have maintained their charm while incorporating rich cultural legacies into vibrant modern communities.

Africa's coastal areas, too, provide a treasure trove of cultural sites that bring the past to life. Consider Zanzibar, an island off the Tanzanian coast steeped in a rich tapestry of Arab, Indian, and African influences. Stone Town, a UNESCO World Heritage Site, with its labyrinthine alleys and spice-filled air, invites exploration. Here, the past remains palpable—each carved door and intricate balcony tells stories of sultans and traders, of a thriving center of commerce and culture.

The coast of Southeast Asia is dotted with sites that capture the spiritual and historical essence of the region. Bali isn't just about its surf-friendly beaches; it's also renowned for its temples and rituals that infuse daily life. The water temple of Pura Ulun Danu Bratan, sitting pristinely on Lake Bratan, offers a serene view that transcends the natural beauty surrounding it, as it serves as a testament to the island's deep spiritual roots.

Further along, Vietnam's coastline is often underestimated. However, it is home to the ancient town of Hoi An, an exceptionally well-preserved trading port dating from the 15th to the 19th century. The blend of history and architecture creates a mosaic of Chinese, Japanese, and European influences visible in its tan-ochre buildings, offering travelers a living museum under the open sky.

In North America, coastal areas such as Mexico's Yucatan Peninsula provide a unique cultural expedition with sites like Tulum. Perched dramatically over the Caribbean Sea, this pre-Columbian Mayan walled city offers insight into the complex society and their profound connection to the cosmos—a connection that continues to resonate with today's visitors who seek more than just a day at the beach.

These cultural sites near coastal regions remind us of the intersection between human ingenuity and the natural world. They're living memorials to our shared history, allowing us to walk paths trodden by those who came before.

In exploring these areas, the journey becomes both an outer adventure and an inner exploration—a reflection on how the ocean shapes not only landscapes but entire cultures. They urge you to step away from the familiar tides and delve deeper into the stories woven into the fabric of these coastal lands. Here, every arch, every weathered stone, and every breath of sea air forms a narrative that invites exploration and reflection, transforming a beach holiday into a cultural odyssey.

As these coastal cultural sites continue to enchant and educate, they also stand as a testament to the resiliency and diversity of human civilization. They ask each traveler to pause, to consider the layers of history beneath their feet and the cultural journeys that extend far beyond the sand and surf. In coastal adventures, these sites offer grounding points, where history and humanity resonate in harmony with the ever-present song of the sea.

Chapter 23:
The Ultimate Beach Bucket List

An intoxicating compendium for the true beach aficionado, "The Ultimate Beach Bucket List" embraces the spirit of exploration with open arms and sandy toes. From the sun-kissed shores of Baja California's hidden enclaves to the serene stretches of sand caressed by the Andalusian tides, this chapter unfurls a tapestry of coastal dreams. Imagine strolling through the crystalline waters of Iceland's pristine fjords or basking under the eternal sun of Seychelles' secluded coves—a beach lover's wonderland teeming with undiscovered allure. You'll discover not only beaches adorned with emerald waters and lustrous sands but also the quiet hum of bays that hold secrets waiting to be unraveled. It's a call to wander, to revel in the tranquil symphonies of crashing waves, and, above all, to cherish the unparalleled beauty that awaits where the land meets the sea. Embark on this curated journey, armed with the promise that somewhere beyond the horizon, your perfect strip of sand beckons you to find it.

Must-Visit Beaches for Every Traveler

The world is peppered with beaches that whisper promises of enchantment to every traveler's soul, beaches that are not just destinations but journeys unto themselves. Each one carries its own unique charm, an allure that beckons with its soft sands and shimmering tides. As you step onto these coastal havens, you're not just visiting a place; you're embarking on an adventure that caresses the senses and leaves an indelible mark on the heart.

Imagine the shores of Anse Source d'Argent in Seychelles, where the granite boulders seem artistically scattered like a masterpiece painted by nature's hand. The pink-hued sands and crystalline waters weave a tapestry of serenity, urging you to lose track of time. This beach is a sanctuary where the whispers of the sea tell tales of relaxation and rediscovery, a place where each sunset feels like the first, painting the skies with hues of romance.

Yet, not all must-visit beaches are defined by their solitude. Copacabana Beach in Brazil thrives on its vibrant energy, pulsing with life's rhythm. Here, the golden sands are a stage where locals and visitors dance the samba, and the scent of fresh seafood mingles with the ocean breeze. Copacabana is an invitation to experience the cultural heartbeat of a city, where the beach is as much about connection as it is about leisure.

Journey across the Pacific to Hawaii's luminous Hapuna Beach. With its wide stretch of perfect white sand bordered by azure waters, it is a vision of paradise come to life. The gentle waves invite swimmers of all ages to frolic in their embrace, and the sunsets here are unparalleled. As day turns to night, Hapuna whispers stories of creation, island myths reflecting in the twilight.

Then there's the mystique of Reynisfjara Beach in Iceland. Defined by its black sands and dramatic basalt columns, this beach is a testament to the earth's raw beauty. A stroll along this shoreline is an adventure into the primal elements, where the crashing waves narrate sagas of Nordic gods and ancient folklore. Enshrouded in mystery and awe, Reynisfjara is a bucket list necessity for those who seek the sublime in nature's contrasts.

The idyllic shores of Navagio Beach, also known as Shipwreck Beach in Greece, tell a different story altogether. Nestled on the island of Zakynthos and only accessible by boat, it's famed for the rusting shipwreck that rests upon its sands. Surrounded by towering cliffs and turquoise waters, Navagio Beach is an ethereal escape that feels suspended in time, a canvas for both adventure and reflection.

Travel southward to the golden expanse of Eleuthera in the Bahamas, home to the renowned Pink Sands Beach. The pale pink sands draw visitors who marvel at this natural phenomenon. It's a place where you can walk along the shoreline with a sense of wonder, each step accompanied by the gentle rhythm of the waves. The beach is not just a place to unwind but a sanctuary to find inspiration and solace in its rosy embrace.

A twist of exotic awaits at Maya Bay in Thailand, made famous by cinema yet still holding a magic that no screen can fully capture. Framed by steep limestone hills and vibrant coral reefs, this protected bay offers a sanctuary for marine life and adventurers alike. The waters of Maya Bay are a living mosaic of blues and greens, each wave inviting you deeper into the beauty of the Andaman Sea.

Across the world, Bondi Beach in Sydney stands as a symbol of Australia's coastal culture. Here, laid-back vibes blend effortlessly with the thrill of surfing. Bondi is not just a beach; it's an icon, a place where life is lived to its fullest, from sun-soaked mornings to lively evenings. Whether you're riding a wave or savoring a meal along the bustling promenade, Bondi offers the quintessential Sydney experience.

At the end of a continent lies the wild, untamed beauty of the Cape of Good Hope in South Africa. Here, the tumult of the Atlantic meets the currents of the Indian Ocean in a dramatic display of nature's grandeur. The beaches around the Cape are not for lounging but for absorbing the awe of a world so grand and textured, a reminder of the earth's dynamic and majestic forces.

Whether you crave the solitude of an untouched cove or the vibrancy of a renowned beach, there's a stretch of sand out there that matches your dreams. These must-visit beaches are touchstones of inspiration, each offering their own stories and experiences. They call us back to the sea's eternal rhythms, urging us to explore, discover, and fall in love with the world anew. So, pack light, tread softly, and let the waves guide your journey to these paradisiacal shores.

Hidden Bays Waiting to be Discovered

Imagine standing on the brink of a secluded bay, a place where time seems to pause in reverence to the natural beauty that exists all around. Such bays, waiting to be discovered, are whispers of tranquility in a world too often submerged in noise. They are the quiet corners of the earth that challenge intrepid explorers to look beyond the usual path and peel back layers of the familiar landscape. As the sun dips below the horizon, these hidden gems sparkle with mystery and promise, inviting those who dare to seek them out.

Each hidden bay has its own story to tell, a rich narrative crafted over millennia by the wind and waves. These places are born of both serenity and tempest, shaped as much by their isolation as by the cultures that have brushed against their sandy shores. In these nooks of nature, history echoes softly, like the gentle lap of the tide against ancient rocks. To wander here is to step back in time, to travel a less beaten path to a world where the heart can feel the pulse of the earth.

In many ways, these bays redefine the very essence of exploration. The adventure lies not in conquering them but in embracing their untouched beauty. They offer solitude to those who seek peace, but for the curious, a hidden bay is a canvas of endless possibilities—a realm for snorkeling, paddling, or simply basking in the sun. It's a place where you can let your thoughts drift away on the gentle breeze, carrying with it the stresses of the world beyond.

Hidden bays are more than picturesque landscapes; they are sanctuaries for wildlife, safe havens for creatures that meld harmoniously with their environment. The still waters harbor vibrant marine life, from playful dolphins to resilient sea turtles. Birdwatchers might spot a rare species flitting across the azure sky, while beneath the surface, vivid coral gardens teem with activity. It's in these quiet enclaves that nature exerts its profound impact, a reminder of the delicate balance that sustains life.

Reaching some of these hidden bays can be a pilgrimage in itself. They often require us to leave behind the predictability of paved roads and town centers, instead embracing the unpredictability of trails, canoes, or small fishing boats that chart courses through jungles and quiet waters. This journey, challenging as it might be, is part of the allure. The more remote the bay, the greater its reward, turning travel into an act of discovery surrounded by the earth's raw, untouched beauty.

In places like Thailand's Andaman coast or the remote isles of Greece, hidden bays present opportunities not only for exploration but for connection. Here, you might find a local fisherman crafting his nets or a quiet village where traditions are preserved as lovingly as the artisanal crafts displayed in narrow, winding streets. Such encounters underscore the deep cultural tapestry that makes each bay distinct, adding personal texture to the geography.

Of course, the discoveries within these bays extend beyond their physical beauty. There's an emotional and spiritual depth that resonates with those who long to disconnect from the rush of daily life. It's in these moments of solitude, standing alone by the water's edge, that one might find clarity. The lapping waves and whispering winds act as nature's symphony, synchronizing with the very heartbeat of those who come seeking solace and serenity.

For couples, hidden bays can set the stage for romance like no other place. With the sky illuminated by a setting sun or a blanket of stars, these places become the backdrop for memories made and promises whispered. They create intimate retreats where love is rekindled and deepened, far from the prying eyes of the bustling world.

Planning a journey to such enchanted places requires more than a map and a guidebook; it calls for an open heart and the willingness to embrace the unexpected. Every bay is a world unto itself, each a different shade of paradise waiting to be unveiled. As you walk along the untrodden path, each step is imbued with the promise of discovery, offering a new perspective on both the world and oneself.

Yet, as more travelers seek these hidden treasures, the need for their preservation becomes paramount. It's crucial to honor the delicate ecosystems and cultural landmarks that make them unique. Responsible travel isn't just a trend; it's a duty to ensure these sanctuaries remain pristine for generations to come. Each visit should echo with respect for the land and its inhabitants, leaving only footprints behind.

In the exploration of hidden bays, travelers are called to redefine their journey, to let go of structured itineraries and embrace the spontaneity of nature's gifts. These bays are a testament to the beauty that lies in the less obvious, encouraging us to delve deeper, explore further, and unearth the extraordinary hidden within the folds of the ordinary world. Whether you've journeyed far and wide or simply dreamt of such adventures from the comfort of your home, these bays captivate and inspire, urging us to listen to the ocean's whispers and to follow where they might lead.

Chapter 24:
Stories of Solitude

In the heart of solitude, there lies an undeniable allure—a certain magic in standing before an unbroken horizon as the waves whisper secrets only the contemplative can hear. This chapter invites you to explore the profound peace found when nature's embrace is your only company. Imagine strolling along a deserted shoreline, where each step imprints stories untold, with the gentle caress of a salty breeze providing a symphony of serenity. Such places offer a refuge from the cacophony of daily life, inviting introspection and a reconnection with one's inner adventurer. Whether it's a remote cove tucked away in New Zealand or a forgotten beach along Africa's Indian Ocean, these secluded escapes promise a deeper understanding of yourself and the world. Here, time slows down, allowing for the kind of reflection that often eludes us. Let your journey through these stories of solitude be both a voyage of discovery and a gentle reminder that the most meaningful adventures are found in the serene solitude of coastal paradises.

The Power of an Uninterrupted Horizon

There's something magnetic about standing at the edge of the world, where land and sea embrace under a vast, unobstructed sky. At the heart of these experiences lies the allure of an uninterrupted horizon, a line where sky meets water in a seamless dance. For travelers seeking solitude, the horizon represents a sense of infinite possibility, a chance to breathe deeply and let the mind roam free.

On secluded shores, time seems to slow to the rhythm of the waves. Here, distractions fade, leaving only the gentle push and pull of the tides. This natural cadence invites a reconnection not just with the world around us, but within ourselves. The horizon, stretching as far as the eye can see, whispers promises of adventure, peace, and an eternal connection to the mysterious beyond.

Imagine the sun casting its golden hues across a tranquil sea, each ripple reflecting its fiery descent. As daylight wanes, the horizon serves as a canvas for the transition from vibrant day to serene night. This daily act of nature's theater creates a moment of introspection, where one can ponder life's greater questions or simply absorb the beauty of the world.

In places untouched by the clamor and bustle of modern life, the solitude found by the sea is profound. These moments of solitude are what draw people to far-flung beaches and hidden bays, where the horizon is a perpetual invitation. The sheer vastness of the ocean is a reminder of our place in the grand tapestry of existence, both humbling and exhilarating.

The power of an uninterrupted horizon is transformative. It nurtures a sense of freedom and peace, offering a respite from the chaos and noise of everyday life. As you stand there, with sandy toes and salt-kissed skin, the horizon becomes a metaphor for life's endless opportunities. It's a gentle nudge, encouraging endeavors and dreams yet to be realized.

We've all read tales of adventurers who write about looking out to an endless sea and feeling a call to explore. There, where the water meets the sky, there's a promise of discovery, of stories yet untold. This invisible line isn't just a boundary; it's a gateway to new horizons, both literally and figuratively.

Every horizon viewed in solitude has the power to stir the soul. Whether it's a wild Atlantic coast where the wind howls and the waves crash, or a placid lagoon shimmering under a midday sun, the effect is the same. There's a magic in the realization that no matter how far you travel, the horizon always awaits, steadfast and unchanged.

For each of us, these moments spent gazing across an endless expanse are personal. They might be shared in silence with a loved one or treasured in solitary reflection. What we find on the other side of the horizon is often a better understanding of ourselves—a discovery of our strengths, our dreams, and our capacity for hope.

A shore, uninterrupted and vast, allows for clarity in a cluttered mind. Decisions that seemed insurmountable become manageable. Stress dissipates with each wave that curls upon the sand. This is the soothing balm that only nature can provide, an antidote to the pressures of modern life.

The horizon is also a haven for dreamers. As night creeps in, stars begin to prick the charcoal sky, each one a wish or a story told by the cosmic universe. Imagine lying on a warm beach as the milky way unfolds above you, feeling small yet significant in the setting of this breathtaking natural cathedral.

In solitude moments meant for embracing, the horizon serves not just as a destination, but a revelation. It encourages personal growth and transformation, urging us to explore not just the world, but the deepest recesses of our inner selves. This quiet communion with the infinite is the sweet spot where imagination and reality blur.

And while these horizons may shift depending on where they are experienced, the essence remains constant. Whether found along a tropical coast with palm trees swaying above the scene, or an isolated cove where rocky cliffs rise majestically from the sea, the power of the horizon lies in its ability to transcend boundaries and spark joy.

Travelers who venture to secluded shores understand the profound effects these places can have. They return with stories in their eyes and the sea in their heart, transformed by the quiet power of an uninterrupted horizon. For it is here, where the land slips gracefully into the sea, that the soul finds its harmony and the spirit its wings.

The horizon's beauty is not just in its views but in its promise—a reminder that there's more world to see, more life to live, and more discoveries just waiting to be made. The lure of the blue, the melody of the waves, and the endless line where sea meets sky all serve to inspire journeys to places unseen, driven by the power found in solitude's embrace.

Finding Peace in Nature's Embrace

Solitude changes us. It strips away the cacophony of our daily lives and fills the void with a different kind of music—the gentle lapping of waves, the whisper of the wind through the pines, the symphony of birds. In these moments, when the world feels still and serene, we find a kind of peace that seems untouched by time. On coastal paths less traveled, amid nature's embrace, we uncover a tapestry of tranquility woven with silence, salt air, and sunlit horizons.

Imagine standing on a deserted beach, where the sand stretches endlessly before you, unmarked by the footsteps of others. The ocean sprawls ahead, an uninterrupted expanse of blue that meets the sky at the horizon, creating an infinite line of possibility. Is there anything more peaceful than witnessing the day break or taking its leave in such an unspoiled setting? Such moments invite reflection and inspire introspection, offering clarity where confusion once thrived.

There's a certain magic found when wandering these secluded shores. Every aspect of life seems to slow, as if the very heartbeat of time syncs with the rhythmic call of the waves. It's an invitation to pause and dream, to let the beauty of the natural world unravel the knots of stress and worry that have tangled within. In these settings, whole lifetimes of tension can seem to melt away with each breath, each gentle step across the powdery sands.

Wild landscapes hold a particular ability to renew the spirit. It's in the sharp scent of salt in the air, mingling with the earthy aromas of coastal vegetation. It's in the sight of sea birds wheeling overhead, their cries sharp and bright against the open sky. For those seeking solitude, the shores become more than just a destination; they transform into sanctuaries where one can reconnect with inner self and the simplicity of the natural world.

At times, the most profound moments occur in silence. Standing alone on a seaside bluff, the only company the sky and sea share is the occasional call of a distant gull. The stillness invites contemplation, a rare luxury in today's fast-paced life. There is power in these quiet moments, in the ability to sit with one's thoughts undisturbed by the hum of technology and obligations. It's here, on the edges of the earth, that the mind can wander freely and reflect on what truly matters.

For the traveler yearning to escape the noise of the everyday, nature's embrace offers an elixir for the senses. Strolling through a dense canopy where sunlight dances through the leaves, or along rocky shores where the surf pounds with ceaseless force, one rediscovers a sense of wonder and awe. Such landscapes are both grounding and liberating—a reminder of the world's beauty and our small, yet significant, place within it.

The windswept dunes of a forgotten coast, the gentle murmur of a secluded bay at twilight, the golden blaze of sunsets that paint the sky in hues of purple and red—all these serve as reminders of the intrinsic beauty that exists beyond the confines of our structured lives. It's a beauty that requires no validation, no curation; it simply is. Such experiences leave an indelible mark, a gentle nudge that perhaps all we really need, at least from time to time, is the solitude that nature provides.

There is adventure, too, in seeking out these serene spaces. The journey to find them often requires a willingness to travel the less-traveled paths, to embrace the unknown with the spirit of exploration. But the rewards are great; discovery itself becomes its own form of contentment. As the ocean spray kisses your face and the sun warms your skin, an inner restfulness quietly grows—a personal sea change. You return from such journeys better for having sought them out, holding tightly to the peace found in those tranquil spaces.

In this space between land and sea, we find reminders of the constancy of change, yet also of enduring stillness. Witnessing the tides' ever-present ebb and flow, we remember that tranquility and chaos can exist in harmony. Life's turbulent times can be endured with grace, much like the unending cycle of ocean waves.

Perhaps, in seeking nature's embrace, we're all looking for a kind of belonging that doesn't bind, but liberates. The places where solitude thrives remind us we're not just visitors in the natural world, but part of its intrinsic rhythm. To know this peace is to come away changed— serene, inspired, and a little more in tune with the world and ourselves.

Chapter 25:
Year-Round Coastal Escapes

Imagine a world where the sand warms your winter-chilled toes, and the summer sun gently kisses your skin no matter the season. This chapter unveils the secrets of coastal destinations that invite you every month of the year, offering beaches that transform their charm with the changing calendar. Whether you're seeking the quiet whisper of waves in a secluded cove during the off-peak splendor of autumn or the vibrant life of a sun-drenched shore in the spring, these year-round escapes are tailored to your adventurous spirit and desire for tranquility. It's here that you'll find moments of ultimate relaxation, far from the throngs of the usual bustling beach crowds, and discover the raw beauty and solitude that paradoxically enlivens and calms the soul. With just a little planning, timing, and curiosity, these coastal paradises promise a unique and enriching escape, tailor-made for every wanderlust heart yearning to explore the timeless allure of the sea.

Best Beaches by Season

Traveling the world in search of stunning beaches is a journey best undertaken with the rhythm of the seasons. Each season paints the coastlines with its unique palette, offering a fresh view and experience around every corner of the globe. Whether you crave the warmth of the sun on your skin or the cool breeze in your hair, there's a beach calling your name at some point in the year. Below is a journey through the best beaches each season has to offer, a canvas of wonders that nature unveils as time turns its wheel.

Spring's Awakening: As the world shakes off the chill of winter, spring breathes life into coastal landscapes. In California, the famed beaches of Santa Barbara bask in the renewed sunshine, where March blooms bring a vivid array of wildflowers to the rugged cliffs. Meanwhile, the Amalfi Coast in Italy is awakening, and travelers can stroll along cliffside paths without the summer crowds, enjoying the scent of blossoming lemon trees mingled with the sea air.

Spring also heralds the ideal time to visit Japan's Okinawa Islands, where cherry blossoms grace the beaches with their ephemeral beauty. The mild temperatures and clear skies provide perfect conditions for snorkeling in reefs teeming with vibrant marine life. It's a season of renewal, where the symphony of gentle waves and the aroma of blooming flora create a pageant in harmony.

In Australia, autumn is falling, but the Great Ocean Road still beckons with its rugged beauty and moderate climate. Golden hues paint the landscape, inviting road trippers to catch the coastal glow of this southern paradise. As you meander through this iconic route, each turn offers a new vista, a reminder that nature writes its poetry not just in florals but also in sands and tides.

Summer's Embrace: As temperatures soar, the world turns to the beach for respite. In this season, nothing beats the Mediterranean's charm. The Greek Islands beckon with azure waters and white-sand beaches. Mykonos, with its vibrant nightlife and serene hidden coves, offers a juxtaposition of excitement and tranquility.

Farther west, Portugal's Algarve Coast is a sun-soaked haven where dramatic limestone cliffs crown golden beaches. Here, the crystal-clear waters invite hours of exploration by kayak or leisure by the shore, promising lazy afternoons with a backdrop of endless blue skies.

Summer is also when the beaches of Hawaii light up with energy. Each island offers its unique flavor—Maui's Kaanapali for families and Kauai's Hanalei Bay for those seeking solitude amid spectacular scenery. Surfers and sun-seekers alike flock to these shores, drawn by the island breezes and aloha spirit.

Autumn's Retreat: As the world slows down, autumn paints beaches in softer colors. The Pacific Northwest, often shrouded in mystery, becomes a surreal landscape of vibrant foliage and dramatic coastlines. Oregon's Cannon Beach, with its famous sea stacks, offers a more contemplative experience as the crowds wane, and the cooler air invites reflective walks along the shore.

Europe's coasts remain alluring—in the south, Spain's Costa Brava extends a quieter charm. Fishing villages, like Cadaqués, reveal their authentic heart during this time, promising rich cultural encounters alongside natural beauty. The warmth lingers, making it ideal for exploring the coastal paths or relaxing at a seaside café.

In Southeast Asia, the Andaman Sea draws travelers to its tranquil shores. Thailand's beaches around Krabi, free from the boom of high season, offer an intimate experience with nature. Kayaking through the limestone karsts and mangroves, travelers find tranquility wrapped in the soft embrace of autumn's retreat.

Winter's Quiet Solitude: For those seeking an escape from winter's grasp, the Southern Hemisphere provides sun-baked escapades. Cape Town's beaches offer a tapestry of white sands and azure waves, set against Table Mountain's commanding presence. Here, each sunset is a masterpiece, a dazzling display of color that warms both the skies and the soul.

The Caribbean is also a winter haven. Turquoise waters and coral reefs call adventurers to the shores of Barbados and the Bahamas, where the rhythm of calypso drifts in the air. It's the season where every coconut palm seems to whisper a welcome of warmth.

For a true winter wonder, the beaches of Bora Bora in French Polynesia provide an escape into a fantastical realm. Overwater bungalows offer a front-row seat to underwater delights, with the inviting lagoon's every ripple a counterpoint to the stillness of the sky. It's a sanctuary where serenity and romance dance a perpetual waltz.

Every season holds its magic, and the world's coastlines are set to shine under their respective lights. Unveiling their distinct characteristics across time, these beaches provide a place for soul-searching, adventure, relaxation, or a mix of all. When seeking a getaway, let the season guide you to a beach where the land meets the sea and your adventurous spirit finds its home.

Off-Peak Travel for Ultimate Relaxation

It's hard to deny the allure of travel during the high season when the world seems to converge on coastal paradises, bustling with energy and excitement. Yet, for those in search of ultimate relaxation, off-peak travel holds a certain magic that's hard to compete with. This hidden charm invites travelers to embrace a slower pace, offering tranquil stretches of sand and sea where one can unwind without the crowd.

Imagine stepping onto a beach that's yours alone; your footprints the only mark on its virgin sands. The horizon is clear, uninterrupted by sun umbrellas or beach towels. Off-peak travel presents this serene picture as coastal destinations shed their summer skin. The idea of 'relaxation' evolves from simply lying on a sunbed to truly immersing oneself in the natural beauty and culture of a place, uninterrupted and unperturbed.

But when exactly is the off-peak season? It varies from one locale to another, influenced by regional climates and tourism patterns. For some coastal havens, it might mean fewer visitors in late spring or early autumn when the weather is still pleasant but the summer rush has waned. In others, the off-peak months might align with the onset of the cooler, perhaps even rainy, seasons. However, these periods often reveal an authentic side of destinations that's sometimes masked in busier times.

There's an undeniable romanticism in exploring coastal paths with only the gentle whisper of waves as company, or finding a quaint seaside café not buzzing with chatter but filled with the hum of local life. These experiences, enhanced by the absence of crowds, allow for deeper connections—with nature, with the place, and even with oneself.

Consider the joys of reduced travel costs as well. Off-peak travelers often find substantial savings on flights and accommodation, which means that dream beachfront villa or charming seaside bungalow suddenly becomes attainable. Imagine sitting on a balcony, morning coffee in hand, watching a misty sunrise over a quiet ocean. It's moments like these that leave the strongest impressions.

Then there's the chance to engage more personally with locals, learning firsthand the ways their seaside communities ebb and flow beyond the tourist season. At markets, fresh produce spills abundantly with the colors and flavors of the region, embodying the culture in every bite. Sea-to-table dining becomes an exclusive culinary journey, easier to appreciate fully when you're not competing for reservations.

Traveling off-peak doesn't mean trading adventure for relaxation. On the contrary, it can lead to unique experiences: fishing with local anglers, participating in cultural festivals not marked in guidebooks, or joining impromptu games of beach soccer with children whose laughter echoes on the breeze. It's a time for spontaneity, where serendipitous encounters become the highlights of your travel story.

The environment benefits, too, from this mindful travel practice. Visiting during off-peak times reduces the strain on local ecosystems and infrastructure, allowing destinations to manage their resources more sustainably. It's a gentle reminder that responsible tourism is mutually beneficial, preserving the beauty of these places for future explorers.

So, what are the strategies to maximize relaxation during off-peak travel? Begin with research. Understanding the specific seasonal patterns and local activities allows you to plan an enriched itinerary. Prioritize immersive experiences over hectic schedules—less is truly more when the goal is relaxation.

Pack a flexible attitude. Off-peak adventures may come with a quirk or two—perhaps a rain shower or a seasonal closure—but these moments are often the catalysts for the best stories. An unexpected rainstorm can lead to a cozy afternoon in a beachside café, just you and your thoughts, perhaps a notebook in hand, dreaming of narratives to tell when you return home.

There's also a certain delight in observing marine life that follows its own calendar. Outside peak tourist seasons, wildlife often returns to areas previously crowded out. Visit a rocky tide pool and witness crabs scuttling about their business, or stroll along a deserted shoreline to glimpse migratory birds resting away from the throngs.

Choosing off-peak travel is akin to selecting a chef's special at a renowned restaurant—it promises something different and exciting, a taste of the place that's unexpected and, perhaps, more genuine. It's embracing the rhythm of nature and the pace of a locale without the filter of tourism spotlight.

Not only do we discover corners of the world less traveled, but we also find parts of ourselves less explored. It's these off-peak moments that bring serenity—not just the kind that lets you rest better at night, but the kind that lodges in your heart, reminding you of the stillness and contentment that the coast, at its unhurried best, can inspire.

Off-peak travel for ultimate relaxation gently beckons us to enjoy the whispering tides, the soft stretch of sunset across the horizon, and the luxury of an unspoken contract with time itself—where you savor moments longer, breathe a little easier, and return home with your spirit lighter.

Conclusion

As we've traversed the sandy pathways and hidden coves of this expansive journey, an undeniable truth has emerged—a profound connection to the world's coastlines enriches not only the body but also the soul. For those who've followed this voyage, the desire to seek and cherish the world's most stunning and secluded coastal paradises has grown exponentially. The adventure is as much about the geography of wonder as it is about a journey into the heart and spirit.

Wandering these remote shores, you've undoubtedly seen how each location offers its own brand of magic. From the azure waters of the Caribbean to the rugged beauty of Northern Europe's coast, each site captures a unique essence that beckons explorers with promises of discovery and solace. While our daily lives are often consumed by the chaos and demands of urban existence, these coastal retreats provide a sanctuary where time slows, and nature's rhythm dictates the day.

Traveling to these paradises is not merely about the pursuit of aesthetics or postcard-perfect moments. It is about reclaiming a part of ourselves that thrives in nature's embrace. Adventure awaits in every corner of the globe, from the vibrant marine life beneath Thailand's tropical waves to the mesmerizing seascapes of New Zealand's tranquil bays. These experiences remind us of our shared human desire to explore, to find, and to understand.

In our quest to uncover these hidden treasures, we find more than just the physical landscapes—it's a reconnection with a deep-seated spiritual and historical tapestry that binds us to these coastal wonders.

Their myths and legends, woven into the fabric of local cultures, enrich our journeys and deepen our understanding that while beaches may seem like mere fringes of land, they're often gateways to profound, time-tested traditions and stories. As you stand on the edge of a forgotten bay or beneath a starlit sky on a secluded beach, you're tapping into a lineage of explorers, adventurers, and dreamers who have been drawn to these shores for centuries.

The healing power of the ocean you've read about here is real and might even be transformative. The calm induced by the rhythmic lapping of waves, the invigorating bite of a salt-tinged breeze, and the endless blue horizon play a role in restoring our mental equilibrium. Each chapter has shown different dimensions of this serenity, emphasizing the idea that there's a certain kind of therapy that can only be offered by the sea, providing us with clarity, inspiration, and peace.

Yet, with every bit of beauty we celebrate, there's also a responsibility we hold as stewards of these coastal treasures. The increase in tourism poses significant challenges, and the book underscores the urgency of balancing enjoyment with preservation. Conservation isn't just a necessity; it's a moral obligation if we are to ensure these paradises remain enchanting for future generations. Sustainable tourism and active conservation efforts are more than just buzzwords; they're the keys to maintaining the delicate balance between human desire and ecological well-being.

While our journey may conclude here within these pages, we stand at the threshold of new beginnings. Equipped with knowledge and inspiration, it's time to carve out your path. Whether it's planning your next getaway to an unexplored beach, engaging in conservation initiatives, or simply spreading the word of these coastal marvels, your connection to these shores doesn't end with the turn of the last page.

In essence, the spirit of the ocean calls to each of us. It whispers promises of journeys yet to come, adventures waiting just beyond the surf. So let us allow the lessons learned, the inspirations gathered, and the stories shared to guide us toward a future that cherishes, respects, and protects the marvels of our coastal wonderlands. As the vast ocean stretches out beneath the sun, endless and eternal, so too may our quest for beauty and serenity continue, with every grain of sand beneath our feet marking another step on the journey.

Appendix A:
Appendix

In pursuit of the untouched and profound beauty that our world's coasts offer, this appendix serves as your compass, directing you toward further enchantment and deeper understanding. Here, you've got a treasure trove of further readings and resources that'll illuminate the pages with more vivid landscapes and stories of the seaside's allure. We extend heartfelt gratitude to those wanderers and dreamers who painted these vivid tales on the canvas of sandy shores and roaring waves. Their journeys and insights infuse this book with authenticity and inspiration, perpetuating the enduring romance of coastal exploration. Immerse yourself in the text, and don't forget to take notice of the authors' backgrounds—their relentless curiosity and passion for coastal wonders form the backbone of your voyage through these pages. Thanks also to the myriad of voices that contributed their stories, offering glimpses into the heart of the ocean's embrace. Consider this appendix your gateway, a simple yet profound reminder that there is always more to discover beyond the horizon.

Further Reading and Resources

As you embark on your own journey to explore the world's most stunning and untouched coastal paradises, expanding your horizons beyond this book can deepen your appreciation and understanding of these incredible places. Below is a curated selection of books, documentaries, and online resources that can serve both as inspiration and as practical guides for further exploration.

For those with a deep love of adventure literature, the works of Patrick Leigh Fermor offer an evocative exploration of travel that's sure to resonate with any wanderer. His vivid prose brings faraway places to life, highlighting not only the natural beauty of landscapes but also the cultural richness that can be found along the shores of foreign lands. His books offer an excellent starting point for cultivating a literary journey around coastal wonders.

If you're captivated by the allure of oceanic life and wish to learn more about the marine environments that influence our shores, consider exploring "The Sea Around Us" by Rachel Carson. This classic work delves into the biology and ecology of the oceans, presenting the wonder of the seas and emphasizing the importance of conservation efforts. Carson's prose is both scientifically informed and beautifully articulated, making complex marine concepts accessible to all readers.

Documentaries can also be an inspiring way to experience the beauty of coastal regions without leaving your home. "Blue Planet II," narrated by Sir David Attenborough, provides breathtaking visuals and compelling narratives about marine life and the environmental challenges facing our oceans today. It's a must-watch for anyone looking to deepen their connection with the aquatic world.

For those interested in the intersection of history and coastal exploration, "The Salt Path" by Raynor Winn offers a poignant memoir chronicling a walk along England's South West Coast Path. This personal journey showcases the healing power of nature and the transformative impact of the ocean, capturing the spirit of adventure and resilience.

If planning your coastal adventure is on your horizon, there are numerous resources available to assist with the logistics. Websites like Lonely Planet and TripAdvisor offer user-generated reviews and tips on visiting less-traveled beaches and secluded bays. They can provide up-to-date information on where to stay, what to see, and how to experience the magic of a locale like a local.

For more practical advice on travel, "Vagabonding" by Rolf Potts provides insights into long-term travel, encouraging readers to embrace the uncertain and thrilling parts of travel, particularly in remote seaside locations. This guidebook combines philosophical reflections with practical tips, making it a useful resource for those venturing into extended coastal explorations.

Cookbooks may not be the first resource you consider, but they can offer fascinating insights into the coastal regions explored in this book. "Sea and Shore: Recipes and Stories from a Restaurateur's Travels" by Emily Scott weaves together stunning recipes and narrative tales gathered from coastal cultures around the world. These cookbooks not only deliver flavors of the sea but deepen your cultural appreciation of maritime communities.

Finally, for those who enjoy a scientific perspective, resources like the National Oceanic and Atmospheric Administration (NOAA) website provide extensive data and research on marine ecosystems, climate change impacts, and conservation initiatives. It's a treasure trove of information for those curious about how our planet's coasts are constantly evolving and the measures we can take to protect them.

For those who find solace in digital wanderlust, platforms such as Instagram and Pinterest allow you to visually explore gemstone beaches and hidden bays around the world through stunning photography. Following travel influencers and photographers can provide daily inspiration and ideas for future trips.

In the end, becoming a true coastal connoisseur is about embracing both the serenity and the complexity of seaside travels. Whether you're looking to expand your knowledge, fuel your dreams, or plan your next escape, these resources can serve as your companions on the journey, guiding you through enchanting shorelines and beyond. The world's coastal treasures await your discovery, and the pursuit of their stories promises endless inspiration and adventure.

Remember, exploration is as much about the journey as it is about the destination. Dive into these resources, let them inspire you, and who knows—your next great coastal adventure might be just around the corner.

About the Authors

Traveling has a way of shaping us, and for the authors of this book, it has certainly carved out a path worth sharing. United by their passion for exploration and a shared love for the sea, they embarked on a journey to capture the essence of the world's hidden coastal gems. On this journey, they've weaved narratives that reflect not only the destinations but also the emotions evoked by these remarkable landscapes.

Our first author grew up by the shores of New England, where the salty breeze and rolling waves kindled a lifelong romance with the ocean. It was more than just scenery; it was solace. Summer days were spent cataloging pieces of driftwood and listening to the whispers of seashells. This love eventually evolved into a pursuit of capturing stories of lesser-known beaches and bays, each with its own unique rhythm and character.

The second author hails from the bustling cities of Europe. An initial career in architecture brought an appreciation for spaces both natural and constructed. Yet, it was a visit to the azure waters of Croatia that kindled a spark for discovering places where nature's architecture took center stage. A journey to understand how people interact with their coastlines became a mission. In places where land meets sea, they found tales of culture, resilience, and wonder.

The third member of this vibrant trio spent formative years exploring the varied coastlines of Asia. Fueled by the rich tapestry of cultures and landscapes found in places like Indonesia and Thailand, their storytelling embodies an unending sense of curiosity and adventure. Countless hours spent under the sun, navigating through narrow lagoons gave them insights into the delicate balance and sheer beauty these secluded paradises hold.

Together, these authors have chronicled vibrant escapades, from secluded Thai islands to the raw elegance of New Zealand's bays. With a tapestry of personal anecdotes and insightful observations, they hope to inspire wanderlust in those yet to visit these corners of the world. Their stories aren't just about the features of the land but about the way these places make you feel and dream.

Behind every chapter lies extensive research, countless conversations with locals, and an endless curiosity for the world. They have gone beyond tourist trails, offering readers secret pathways and local wisdom. This trio brings an unmatched insight by drawing upon diverse backgrounds and experiences, crafting a narrative that is both deeply personal and universally relatable.

In this book, the authors have skillfully combined their individual talents and perspectives to encourage readers to seek the roads less traveled. By highlighting the harmony and mystery of these coastal destinations, they celebrate the endless romance between land and sea. Whether you're setting sail for new shores or browsing for inspiration from home, their words are an invitation to explore with eyes wide open.

Yet, beyond the sandy beaches and sparkling waters, the authors emphasize respect and preservation. They are storytellers, yes, but advocates too, fostering awareness of the impacts of tourism and the importance of sustainability. Each visit, they argue, should be responsible, ensuring these paradises remain pristine for future generations.

Above all, the authors weave an invisible string of connection. Their tales are reminders of shared sunsets, universal nostalgia, and the profound peace that only an uninterrupted horizon can deliver. Each chapter is a call to both adventure and reflection, to discover not just the world's coastal paradises but perhaps a little more about oneself in the process.

To all readers embarking on this journey through these pages, the authors simply ask you to carry a reverence for nature and a heart wide open to the beauty of discovery. A hidden beach somewhere will always have space for someone willing to find it. In these tales, the authors deliver the promise of adventure, a whisper from the sea, and a guidebook to the soul of coastal paradises.

Acknowledgments

Certain journeys in life leave footprints not just on the path but on one's soul. This book was such a journey, where each page turned into a new horizon and not possible without the dedication and support of many. First, we express our deepest gratitude to the explorers who ventured into uncharted coasts and returned with tales of wonder and imagery that breathed life into these chapters. Your narratives turned ideas into reality, transforming raw landscapes into destinations of dreams.

To the local communities residing in the paradises scattered across the globe, thank you for sharing your stories, culture, and knowledge about these hidden gems. Without your hospitality and openness, our understanding of these coastal escapes would remain superficial. You've enriched our spirits with your traditions and your unwavering commitment to preserving the natural beauty around you.

The contributions from environmental scientists and marine biologists have been invaluable. Their insights into the delicate balance of marine ecosystems and the impact of tourism have guided us towards advocating for responsible travel. They reminded us that with every wave and tide comes a responsibility to protect and cherish the blue heart of our planet.

Our heartfelt thanks go out to the photographers who captured the essence of each location. Your ability to freeze time in a single frame allowed readers to experience the warmth of the sunlit sands and the whisper of the ocean breeze without physically being there. The power of your art enhanced the narratives, giving each story a visual heartbeat.

We are grateful to the adventurers and travelers who shared their personal tales of solitude and discovery. Your experiences highlighted the profound impact of nature on the human spirit and invigorated our mission with your courage and curiosity. Through your eyes, we saw the true magic of the world's deserted shores and vibrant coastal communities.

Special appreciation goes to the creative team behind this work—the editors, writers, and designers. Your tenacity in ensuring that every detail aligned with our vision did not go unnoticed. Your skill transformed ideas into a cohesive narrative and polished rough drafts into the poignant prose that fills these pages.

We also extend our gratitude to the publishers who believed in the concept and provided a platform to showcase this work. Your belief in the transformative power of travel literature is what brought this project to fruition, allowing us to share it with enthusiasts across the world.

And to our families and friends, thank you for your unwavering support and patience. Your understanding as we embarked on this journey across tides and time zones means more than words can express. You are our anchors, making it possible to chase winds and whims in pursuit of stories worth telling.

Lastly, to the reader, although anonymous here, your unseen encouragement is the silent force propelling us onward. Your thirst for new adventures and experiences fuels our own, pushing us to venture further and dream bigger. May you find inspiration and solace within these pages, and may they guide you to your own unspoiled paradises waiting beyond the horizon.